"Marnie has a unique perspective on an MSP market that needs fresh new ideas—this book is a MUST READ for any MSP owner."

—CHRIS WISER, *CEO, 7 Figure MSP*

"With so many owners of MSPs coming from a technical background, it's understandable some would think just good service is enough. It isn't. Moving beyond just the basics to a process is hard without guidance... and here is the book that is exactly what it says it is. Address the need directly with this spot-on resource from Marnie and the team at Lifecycle Insights."

—DAVE SOBEL, *Host, Business of Tech Podcast*

"Simple, actionable steps to transform your MSP into a 'Managed Success Provider'."

—RAY ORSINI, *CEO, OIT VoIP*

"In her characteristic good humor and down-to-earth wisdom, Marnie hits it out of the park with this primer on Customer Success. A practical, proactive, and insightful guide, Literally the Book on Customer Success for MSPs is packed with useful, foundational knowledge for any business looking to grow."

—ELIZABETH COPELAND, *HelpDesk Buttons*

"This book is a must-read if you want to keep the customers you have, build a stronger, more sticky relationship with them and offer more business value. *Literally* helps to build a process around your MSP company to create or strengthen your Customer Success program and ultimately your business."

—HOWARD GLOBUS, *CEO, IT-On-Demand*

"Clients today expect a higher level of service. This book explains how to provide that extra service to increase revenue per customer, reduce churn and most of all, avoid negative surprises!"

—STEVE KAZAN, *CEO, Inner Onion*

"If you are not meeting with your clients, *now* is the time to start. As an MSP owner for over two decades, I can confidently say that QBRs are one of the keys to our continued success. This book offers the MSP a pragmatic, insightful, and practical approach to begin building your QBR process. If you are looking for ways to increase client retention and referrals and reduce churn, I recommend you read this book."

—LISA SHORR, *Co-Owner Secure Future Tech Solutions*
Image and Brand Expert, Shorr Success

"You can have the tools, and you can have the talent—but they're nothing without drive or a spark of passion behind them, and that's just what this book provides."

—MATTHEW FOX, *Creative Director,*
Valiant Technology

"Brilliant. Actionable. Measurable. Highly recommended for any technology service provider!"

—JENNIFER BLEAM, *Owner & Founder*
MSP Sales Revolution

"*Literally* is literally the playbook on how to align your success with your customers' success. The frameworks will set you apart from your competitors. If you don't want to sprint to the bottom of the pricing race, give this approach a try."

—DAN CALIN, *Program Lead*
Growth Accelerator

"Customer Success, I believe, can be summed up by demonstrating to a client that you care and that it is not all about the 'sale.' A QBR done right can do just that. Lifecycle Insights has provided a tool that allows me to do that."

—RON COTSOPOULOS, *CEO*
Kobus

"I wish I'd had a playbook like this when I first started out managing a Customer Success team! Simple, clear, with a sense of humor—the book can get anyone started with a practical plan that has immediate business impact."

—JUSTIN SERRANO, *CEO*
Littera

"She walked the walk and talked the talk. And now she has written it down. Dr. Stockman has taken complex Customer Success concepts and grounded them for practical application. *Literally* is one of the best tools in your toolkit to reduce churn and drive further adoption and growth in your customer base."

—JUSTIN MILLER, *VP of Customer Success*
eVisit

Foreword by Nigel Moore **of The Tech Tribe**

LITERALLY THE BOOK ON CUSTOMER SUCCESS FOR MSPs

Marnie Stockman, Ed.D.

Year of the Book
135 Glen Avenue
Glen Rock, PA 17327

Print ISBN: 978-1-64649-211-4
Ebook ISBN: 978-1-64649-212-1

CONTENTS

FOREWORD

Since starting in the MSP and IT Support world two decades ago, I've seen our industry go through a number of radical shifts and transformations (aka upgrades).

The first big shift was from Break/Fix to Managed Services as the predominant business model. This is where we moved from Ad-Hoc billing to primarily Monthly Fixed Price Agreements.

The second big shift was from On-Prem to Cloud, where we moved our clients' workloads from SBS and Exchange Servers at their offices to platforms like Microsoft 365 and Google Workspace.

In both of these industry shifts (upgrades), I noticed two primary groups of MSPs owners.

The first bunch were the MSP Business owners who "got it." They saw the writing on the wall that the coming shift was inevitable and they intentionally chose to ride the wave, enjoying and profiting from the fruits of the upgrade. You could call them the "wise" early adopters.

The second bunch were the laggards. They blindly assumed each shift was not going to be permanent and if they kept their heads in the sand long enough, things would stay as they were. Lots of the laggards were simply complacent and apathetic (fancy words for lazy), not seeing the incoming headlights of the freight train of change headed in their direction.

Some of the laggards even chose to actively fight against the shifts. I can't count the number of times I heard:

*"Clients don't need Managed Services,
Break/Fix is much better"*

*"The Cloud is a fad, it won't last,
on-prem is here to stay"*

We all saw what happened in both those cases.

When I had my MSP, we were (semi) early adopters in both of these shifts, moving to a Fixed Fee Managed Services Model and offering Cloud Services quite early.

And, while I could tell you that I made these decisions because I was smart and had the wisdom to spot trends, I'd be blatantly lying. ☺

The reason we were early adopters in both those shifts was because I was addicted to shiny red objects and the allure of new technologies pulled me along. Pure luck, not wisdom, helped me ride those two waves.

However, when I look back now on those two industry shifts, there are obvious patterns, tell-tale signs, and numerous clues that hinted that these shifts were going to be both vastly important and here for the long term.

Right now (in late 2021), I'm seeing those exact same patterns and hints emerge as part of a new shift (upgrade) that our industry is starting to go through.

This particular shift sees us moving away from technology being the core of an MSP's offering and toward Customer Success and Client Experience as the centerpiece. A shift where MSP offerings are built and managed with the Client Experience at the core and the technology being only a minor piece of the pie.

It's a much more subtle shift than Break/Fix to MSP or On-Prem to Cloud. However—in my (not so humble) opinion—the table stakes are *much* higher this time around because of two major forces that didn't exist during those previous two big shifts.

Firstly, there are now a bunch of MSPs that are 15-25 years old (some even older). These MSPs have had decades to build and improve their systems, grow their teams and build their client bases. They have very mature sales systems, marketing engines, and service delivery teams. They are maturing more and more every day and the gap between them and newer entrants is widening.

This gap makes it hard for newer (or lower maturity) MSPs to compete against these highly mature MSPs, as their people, processes, and offerings have been improved and refined now over decades.

And secondly, there are more and more MSPs starting up every day than ever before (despite the tough, mature competition). Some would say this is the societal shift of people wanting to take their destiny in their hands by starting and owning their own business.

There were tell-tale signs and numerous clues that hinted that these shifts were going to be vastly important and here for the long term.

These two forces, made up of the mature MSPs growing ever more mature and the escalating rise of new entrants to the MSP industry, are making it infinitely harder to compete and market in the growing sea of same-ness. Especially so for the MSPs that differentiate purely from a Product perspective only—that is, by adding more features, or reducing their prices to try and stand out. This differentiation is hard.

So, when Marnie mentioned that she was writing a book to (literally) help MSPs move the needle on Customer Service and Client Experience, I was *excited*. Not only because someone was finally writing on this wildly important and timely topic, but more importantly because it was Marnie doing the writing.

Marnie is one of those humans who, from the first moment you meet her, it's abundantly obvious that she's deeply passionate and wildly wise on the topic of Customer Success and lives and breathes it at an almost abnormal level. Just the type of person you want to listen to and learn from.

And this book is chock full of wisdom and a framework for MSPs to know what to do and how to do it if they want to ride this next shift in the MSP space.

So my encouragement to you here is simple.

Don't be a laggard, secretly hoping you'll be able to survive (let alone thrive) without making any investment into your Customer Success and Client Experience.

And don't be me, blindly chasing red shiny objects, making it through this shift only by pure luck.

Instead, be the informed and wise MSP owner, spotting the trend, and start building a strategy with the help of Marnie's framework to ride the wave that comes with it.

Smart MSPs will start heavily and consistently investing more time and money into their Customer Service and Client Experience and will see *big* dividends. They'll see cheaper marketing costs, they'll close deals faster, they'll win in bidding scenarios more often, they'll differentiate easier, and they'll increase their client retention and referrals. All the juicy stuff every MSP owner wants.

The laggards will get left behind, wondering where the industry and their clients went.

If you're a small ~~nimble~~ MSP, start small and with the basics, knowing that the full framework you learn in these pages is something for you to grow into. If you're a larger (or more mature) MSP, get the ball rolling to implant Marnie's full framework into your teams and business now.

Start riding the shift by becoming an MSP that truly puts Customer Success and Client Experience front and center. Your future clients, team, and self will thank you for it. Onwards and upwards!

Nigel Moore
Founder of The Tech Tribe
Former MSP Owner

P.S. A word of warning (and Marnie might stop being my friend for saying this, haha), but parts of this book are going to be tough work for you. You're going to want to give up and switch across to the next red shiny object or social media feed for another quick-fix of dopamine.

But don't.

There's a reason those parts are tough and it's because they shine a spotlight on things deep down you know you need to be doing and thinking about, *but haven't been.* That spotlight is going to be uncomfortable. But persist, because the outcome on the other side will be worth it!

AUTHORS NOTE:

Nigel can't shake me that easily ☺ and I agree. Some of the work feels like just that—work. If everyone easily skated through the work, it wouldn't be a differentiator. I am grateful to Nigel for calling out the elephant in the room.

INTRODUCTION

"Way to take knives in the back."

*"I heard you were catching bullets
with your teeth."*

These were the Slack messages I received after a week of work.

I was not at a Marine Corps bootcamp. I was not a gladiator. I was not training for *American Ninja Warrior*.

I was a Customer Success Manager.

While I appreciated the recognition for taking one for the team and helping recover an account in jeopardy, I really was more interested in success than heroic feats of bravery. I was also not sure what I had gotten myself into. Having just come from the world of education, where I had been a teacher and administrator, this was not what I expected in the world of Software Development. I felt like I was in a constant game of catch-up or whack-a-mole, fighting fires as they came up. And they came up a lot.

Since I am writing this book on Customer Success as co-founder and CEO of a software platform for managed service providers (MSPs), you can see I survived those knives in the back. But before we get to the happy ending, let me take us back to the beginning.

I am often asked how a high school math teacher landed in the realm of SaaS (Software as a Service) for MSPs. My first comment is always that teachers are naturals at customer success, sales, and marketing. Need proof? Have you ever tried to pitch pre-calculus to a group of 16-year-olds? Or imagine the balancing act of keeping students engaged, parents happy, and test scores that keep administrators pleased. Like I said—naturals.

It felt like I was in a constant game of whack-a-mole.

These skills landed me in administration. My own kids would tell you that my best stories come from being a high school assistant principal. But it was my experience as a math supervisor and accountability coordinator that really fueled my fire. In these roles, I was responsible for the digital transformation of assessment, data collection, and reporting for the school system. We did that by implementing an assessment and analytics platform that transformed the speed at which we could make an impact on student performance. The platform automated data collection and made easy-to-read insights for quick action.

I was so passionate about the impact the platform had for students that I would present it to other school systems. In one of those presentations sat the founder of that software company. He walked me to my car afterward and asked if I would join their customer success team to help their other customers become the same raving fans that I was.

And now we're back to where we started... less than a month later, I was "catching bullets with my teeth." Because I truly believed in the power of the product, I was determined to make it work. But that would take time. First I would have to recover 20 accounts which hadn't been communicated with for 18 months.

A couple months later, when I finally did come up for air, I had lots of opinions on what customer success should and *should not* look like. (Let's be honest, I have always had lots of opinions, but now I also had tons of experiences to support them.)

From those first weeks as a Customer Success Manager to becoming a Senior Director of Customer Success who battled through four acquisitions fighting to do right by our customers, I learned many valuable lessons. Those lessons proved to equate to a retention rate over 95% for a client base of $20+ million dollars in annual recurring revenue (ARR).

Those lessons also led to these strongly-held beliefs that Customer Success teams need:

- An understanding of our customers' businesses
- "English-to-English" translators to advocate for the customer and for our company
- Power and flexibility to get the customer what they need
- Processes to ensure the customer feels heard
- Metrics to ensure progress toward our goals

Our team was a group of rock stars. They knew their stuff, they knew their clients, and they were true partners. They were also expensive. And as the people themselves handheld their clients so much, the people became a part of the product—a well-loved part, but a part that wouldn't scale.

Like a team of actual rock stars, it was very much every person for themselves. They were so swamped with completing tasks that they didn't have time to work *on* the business as they were already drowning in it. Thankfully, my confidante in the company believed in success and was in charge of support. So with the same objective and passion for problem solving, we worked to overhaul our Customer Success program.

We knew we needed a process that was:

- Scalable
- Repeatable

- Documentable
- Efficient

And most important:

- Based on metrics

As it stood, if a Customer Success Manager (CSM) was hit by a bus or left the company, nearly every bit of their client base would be left rudderless and not set up for success.

We decided we needed to approach Customer Success in four steps:

1. Segment our customer base
2. Determine customer health metrics
3. Utilize a means for identifying opportunity
4. Define a process—and see which steps of the process could be automated

That confidante (foreshadowing–who is now one of the co-founders of Lifecycle Insights) and I put people, processes, and products in place. We built a Customer Success program to support that ed-tech analytics company. In doing so, we realized we were passionate about that process and wanted to build a company of our own to grow raving fans.

The next part of the story sounds like the start of a good joke:

"A guy and a girl walk into a bar..."

I was the girl. The guy was an owner of an MSP and we had just finished playing volleyball. I explained our interest in starting a company that could help MSPs grow their businesses and asked him if there were any problems around data in the MSP space. I really didn't see the rant coming. But it started with:

"Spent 8 hours today... cobbling together QBR reports... PSA... RMM... Warranty look-ups... user data..." and ended with "All that time and I still have an ugly report to present to my clients at their business review tomorrow." And then "Can you help with that?"

Several Zoom calls and hours of research later, the three of us decided "Yes! We could!" So Lifecycle Insights was born—a platform to automate QBR reporting, provide flexible assessments, and present pretty reports to help MSPs sell to execs not techs.

As Lifecycle Insights grew, we learned more and more about the roles of account managers, Customer Success Managers, vCIOs, sales, CEOs, and one-man (or woman) shows for MSPs. While we were solving the problem of business reviews for them, we could see another need. As their businesses grew (definitely a side-effect we have seen at Lifecycle Insights), we heard more and more requests that they needed help with Customer Success.

That is not to say our MSP partners were not successful with their customers. They very much were and are. So much so that their businesses grew and needed help scaling. And all MSPs will tell you that to scale anything, you need a process (and a product). So... that brings us to today, where we are literally writing the book on Customer Success for MSPs. (Do I hear *documentation,* anyone?)

> *As MSPs grow, their need for Customer Success expands too*

There are lots of books, blogs, and videos on Customer Success, but typically they focus on departments, divisions, titles, or CRM platforms. The focus for this book is different. We focus on *actual customer success!* We concentrate on the people, program, process, and product that will help you make a positive impact for your customers. Their success guarantees your MSP's success.

This book also focuses strictly on Managed Service Providers (MSPs). Every industry has a role of Customer Success, but the role of an MSP is unique. And that role might be one of many an individual has as their responsibility.

So, right out of the gate, we acknowledge that this book is not for everyone. But if you are a one-person MSP, a member of a small to mid-sized MSP, or part of a larger organization where you are responsible for Customer Success and have asked, "How do I know Customer Success is working for us and our customers?" Then this book is for you.

We see a variety of organizational models and titles throughout the space. Two of the most popular roles that address Customer Success are Account Managers (AMs) and virtual Chief Information Officers (vCIOs). The actual role of Customer Success Manager (CSM) is becoming more popular as the focus on customer outcomes is so strongly linked with driving business for the customer and the MSP.

Many times Customer Success is one of many responsibilities for a sole owner or small MSP where team members play multiple parts. In this book, we simplify the alphabet soup of acronyms and use the term CSM. Understand that we are speaking to the person or persons responsible for engaging with customers to ensure their customer health, their renewal, and their sales opportunities.

Focus on actual customer success...

because your customers' success guarantees your success.

In the case where this role is one of many for a single team member, we help you define a program to buy back some of your time and/or prepare to hire your first CSM. If you are an owner of a larger company or one of many CSMs at your organization, we help you build a consistent process that scales (and sells) across your team.

But most important, we guide you through defining a program to grow Raving Fans![1]

So as we get ready to dive in, we are going to walk through:

1. **The Why**

   The value a Customer Success program brings to your MSP and your customers

2. **The How**

   The steps you need to take to have the right processes in place to scale success

3. **The What**

   The vision for Customer Success done right

This is not your grandmother's account management program. This is *Literally: The Book on Customer Success for MSPs*.

---

[1] If you haven't read the book *Raving Fans: A Revolutionary Approach to Customer Service* by Ken Blanchard, put it on your list. And if you don't have a list, by the end of this book, you will! I absolutely share many of the resources, connections, and people who have shaped my view of Customer Success, along with the personal experiences/mistakes that got us to this point.

PART 1
THE WHY

CHAPTER 1

THE KEY TO SUCCESS

The phone rings. It's Michael, the CEO of one of Kerrie's accounts. Kerrie hasn't heard from the company in a while and is glad to have the opportunity to check in. Not far into the small talk, Michael interrupts. "Sorry to cut you short, Kerrie, but I just wanted to let you know that we won't be renewing our contract. We are going with a new MSP."

Kerrie is speechless—completely blind-sided. She hadn't heard from them recently, but there didn't seem to be any concerns. They had not entered tickets and they hadn't had any downtime. Dread. And now she would have to explain to her boss what had happened.

If this has happened to you—or you fear it could happen to you—then you are in the right place.

Customer Success (CS) plays a vital role in the world of MSPs today. Whether CS is one of the many hats you or someone at your MSP wears, or is a single person dedicated to the role, this person is responsible for the relationship with your customers. This includes making sure your own company isn't blind-sided by phone calls like the one Kerrie received. Done well, Customer Success is extremely rewarding for the Customer Success Manager (CSM), the MSP, and their clients. Done poorly, an undeveloped or non-existent Customer Success program feels like a battleground.

It took me a long time to write these next few sentences. I struggled to find the words that would convey the power of Customer Success, its importance, and its priority for any thriving business. And then I realized why I was having the struggle. It feels like CS should be common sense, but as the saying goes, "Common sense ain't all that common."

So as the typical nerd that I am, I've decided to communicate the message with statistics. The stat we often hear bandied about in the space is that a happy customer tells one friend where an unhappy customer tells ten.

Here are some other statistics on the topic:

- 80% of customers say the experience they have with a company is as important as its product or service (Salesforce.com)

- 76% of companies say they expect a partner to understand their needs and expectations (Salesforce.com)

Read those two statements again. They are *not* actually saying the same thing, yet they are both talking about Customer Success. The first Salesforce quote speaks to the experience itself—how a customer feels about working with you. I have no doubt that you have plenty of evidence that your customers enjoy working with you and/or your team. We often read on MSP websites:

That is certainly part of Customer Success, but it is only a part.

Now, let's look at the second Salesforce stat. This one points to the fact that customers expect their partners to understand their business needs and expectations. This means your MSP better help them meet their business goals or they will take that business elsewhere. At the very least, not doing this devalues the relationship and their goal shifts to finding a way to pay less for your products and services.

A true real-world example:

There came a time (and many of you may relate) when I had to buy a minivan. Let's be clear. I didn't want to buy a minivan, but the daily carpool required it.

In general, I find any experience of buying a vehicle terrible, regardless of how nice, thoughtful, or gracious the salesperson is. "Pleasant" is not something I am looking for while buying a minivan. A *minivan* is what I am looking for.

On this particular day, it was pouring rain. My husband and I drove around the dealership lot with two car-seated kids in tow. I hopped out and checked the sticker price and features on a few minivans, then we headed inside to buy the one I picked out.

> *Customer Success should be common sense... but "common sense ain't all that common"*

We told the salesperson we wanted to buy that minivan. He said, "Well, let me get you to test-drive it."

A debate ensued. It ended with me saying, "Look, I don't *want* to buy this minivan, but I *am* going to buy it. I suspect it drives exactly like my parents' of the same make and model. So if you want me to buy this minivan, then skip the test-drive and process the paperwork."

I realize now that what I was trying to tell him was that I wasn't interested in a great car-buying experience, just the outcome. This is the exact same issue that is missing from many customer success programs and products—a focus on the outcomes.

A pleasant customer experience should be table-stakes. The differentiator is having a program, process, and product to provide insights around growing success for your customers' businesses.

Are you wondering how helping their business is going to help your business? Let's see!

Customer Success is often an afterthought. Frequently MSPs rely on relationships as they grow, so there is no formal CS program. Customer Success tracking is frequently based on instinct instead of information and metrics. It is also sometimes seen as a cost center as opposed to the growth engine that it is.

But let's run the numbers:

> *Industry consultants have shared client results that support the statement that without a Customer Success program that delivers regularly-scheduled business reviews, you are leaving about 30% more monthly recurring revenue (MRR) on the table.*

Calculate that number real fast.

Your current monthly recurring revenue
+ 30% additional revenue
_____
More money!

If you add 30% more revenue to an MSP that is bringing in $750k, in ARR, a CSM adds approximately $225k annually.

> *CSMs often forget to focus on the outcomes*

In the world of no-brainers, this program pays for itself. ROI (Return on Investment) positive. That is before we even consider how CSMs reduce churn and increase referrals.

Whether you are thinking, "We could do better" or *"We could really do better!"* you need to start somewhere. Grabbing this book is a good place to start. In the chapters that follow, we will outline actionable steps you can take to improve your program immediately.

A fair question to ask is: "What happens if I don't?"

Let me pose two additional questions.

> "Are you able to take a real vacation without having to worry about a problem only you can solve?"

> "Are your competitors doing this?"

As we walk through the stages of defining, refining, and scaling a Customer Success program, you will see not only the efficiencies it puts in place for businesses but also how it creates value in terms of referrals, upsells, and raving fans.

Whenever I get overwhelmed with a large project ahead, I like to remind myself: "Done is better than perfect. And perfect is never done." So as we move ahead, just ask yourself: "What is one more thing you can do to add value to your Customer Success program?" If you follow a process of continuous improvement where you move the needle on one component at a time, you will stack a successful pile of *Done* items that lead to significant improvement.

Now that we are ready to roll, let's take a quick step back and look at where we might find roadblocks. As with any situation, the first step in solving a problem is acknowledging you have one.

In the next chapter we'll dig into some of those challenges of CS. Then we can look at a framework for solving them.

Takeaways

- The numbers show a Customer Success program is a must

- Customer Success roles looks different in every MSP ranging from a portion of one person's job to a team of CSMs, vCIOs, and AMs working together

- CS should have documented a program, process, and product that drives customer outcomes/goals

- If you aren't tracking your CS program, your competitors will (and you won't see them coming)

- Start somewhere and iterate

- If 80% of customers are buying based on how they experience Customer Success with a company, then make it your competitive advantage

- Customer Success should help demonstrate the value of the investment your customer has made

CHAPTER 2

IDENTIFYING THE CHALLENGES

Paul is an MSP business owner. He started 15 years ago as a break-fix shop. He was known as Johnny on the spot. He was quick to respond to clients and provided quality service. His business grew by word of mouth. Everyone loved him and he loved helping everyone. He provided the white glove service they wanted and he happily gave everyone his cell phone number.

As the company grew, he started to stress out about the 24/7 workload with all of the phone calls he was handling. Paul was completely burned out. He couldn't handle any more work and things were starting to slip. He couldn't get back to all of his customers in a timely fashion. They started to complain. A few started going elsewhere.

It is common sense where this CS problem comes from. And oddly enough it comes from the best intentions. Paul's story is not unique. Your efforts to grow raving fans can present problems. They can't see what you are doing on the back end to help them, so your over-work may look like you are under-communicating. You must bring your process to light or your customers will be left feeling like they are in the dark. As is so often the case, Paul's strength—great personalized customer service—turned into his weakness.

This dichotomy—where a strength turns into a weakness—is quite typical. Let's talk about two very common strengths we see across many Managed Service Providers.

Strength 1: Automation Rules

Managed Service Providers are the reigning champs when it comes to automation. My business partner who ran an MSP had a sign above his desk that read:

If you have to do something twice, automate it.

So the irony was not lost on him that his entire business review process (which is the foundation of any great Customer Success program) was done manually. Clearly that led to the development of Lifecycle Insights. Our mission was to automate as much of the QBR reporting as possible.

Let's face it. That's not an insanely bold statement: "Automate as much as possible." If we were trying to appeal to MSPs' appreciation of automation, we would have said: "We aim to automate your entire QBR process." So why didn't we? Because that would have been the moment we turned the strength of automation into a weakness. Initially that might hurt some feelings, but hear me out.

It is no surprise in the industry that a great deal of managed service delivery is being commoditized. Technology helps businesses run more effectively, efficiently, and profitably. But if 100% of my interactions with a company can be done without human communication, then I will certainly purchase the cheapest solution. Suddenly, it would be a race to the bottom for MSPs.

You must bring your process to light,
or else your customers will be left
feeling like they are in the dark

If you are confident that your MSP provides business value to your customers in terms of their business outcomes because of your strategic partnership, then do not let your strength (automation) turn into your weakness (commoditization).

People want to do business with people. A Customer Success program helps you define the human element of your business. One of the critical factors of your CS program will be to clearly define those human interactions. Even better (more foreshadowing...) we will define metrics to automate insights so you will know when to take action. This means a Customer Success product will strike the right balance between automation and human partnership.

> *If every interaction with your customer could be automated, it would become a race to the bottom in terms of price*

Strength 2: Customers love you

When I ask MSPs why they started their business, here is a very typical response:

> *"I love all things technology and I want to help people/businesses."*

That was definitely true of Paul, our MSP owner who was so good at customer service that he was drowning in his own business.

That is not the only problem that can arise by having great personal relationships with your customers though. Another problem is that you begin to rely too much on your gut instinct. If you are thinking, "Well, my gut is usually right," then my question for you is: "How do we scale your gut?"

If your immediate response is "With pizza," I believe I have some memes you would appreciate. But as we have already mentioned, if you don't have a process in place that scales, then vacations and work-life balance are near impossibilities. If you think about Kerrie, who thought everything was okay with her customer because she hadn't heard from them, you know that something is missing in the program.

Squishy or missing metrics

Once Kerrie was blind-sided by the news that Michael's company was leaving them, think about what she might have heard if she asked for the reason.

> *"We haven't heard from you recently and everything seems to be running fine so we probably don't need you.*
>
> *When we do hear from you, it's just to make us spend more money. We're not really seeing an ROI for the expense.*
>
> *This other company said they can provide the same products and services cheaper."*

No matter which of those Kerrie heard, it begs several questions:

1. How was Kerrie showing that their MSP services contributed to, or increased, the health and growth of Michael's business technology or the growth of the business as a whole?

2. How was Kerrie partnering with them to deliver an IT budget forecast and strategize as part of their team?

3. How was Kerrie able to connect the business pains they were solving with their IT spend?

Let's look at the same scenario from the perspective of the MSP that Kerrie works for. In reflecting on this call, Kerrie's boss might have had these questions of Kerrie:

- What was their sentiment at their last check-in or business review?

- Were they at risk for churn?

- What impact does this have on our book of business?

- How aligned were they to our business practices?

- Were there any red flags that would have helped us see this coming?

If you or Kerrie can't answer those questions quickly, then you understand the problem of squishy or missing metrics. Kerrie probably has some hunches to answer these questions, but how well are they documented? How consistent are they? How are they regularly monitored?

Many companies rely on their consistently high retention rates to justify why they don't have official documented metrics. That assumption (aka very squishy metric) is dangerous for both the CSM and the MSP. The CSM struggles to quantify their challenges and successes which makes their job seem insecure. Then when the only visible tracking of their work is how much money was expensed to provide coffee for a client's business review, it definitely feels questionable.

For the MSP, the role of CSM without metrics and process is not repeatable and scalable. And without those metrics, how can you establish the impact they have on the business? In Part Two, we are going to detail the metrics to help shore up a Customer Success program which is better business for everyone.

The customer is not always right

There is the unwritten (and sadly sometimes written) rule: The customer is always right. *Oof.* That does *not* set anyone up for success.

Henry Ford of Ford Motors was known for saying: "If we gave everyone what they asked for, we would have built a faster horse."

As I write this, I am thinking of dozens of examples of businesses who land in the situation where they feel their customer's perspective has to be true. This can actually cause more Customer Success problems.

People pleasers, those who are in Customer Success roles to help others, sometimes fall victim. But there are lots of

Having boundaries, policies, and best practices in place are vital for both the MSP and the customer

ways customers are not always right. This is definitely a challenge for a CSM. Having boundaries, policies, and best practices are vital for building the business *and* supporting the customer.

Here are two stories to demonstrate the point.

The $1.4 million dollar deal

On day one of my CSM position, I was sent onsite to our second largest client for their first day of onboarding. Their $1.4 million dollar contract was a big win. They were important. They were influential. The company knew it. I knew it. They knew it.

They were pleased with our services. They had a grand vision on how technology was going to simplify their systems, taking workloads off of people, and getting actionable data into the hands that needed it.

As their dream grew, so did their vision of our technology. They were big and influential, they had great ideas, and I was new and eager to support them. Many times in those first few months, I talked with support or our engineers to do special favors. "They are a big customer. They are an important customer. They know best."

These favors continued to happen. I would hear, "Can your service do...?" If I said no, the response would be, "We paid $1.4 million dollars for this? It should!" I would run the message up the flagpole and folks would pause other projects to work on this one. But soon the message grew stale. Even more importantly, it grew to be a distraction. It pulled us away from our core work. Plus, if we spent all of our time doing custom work, none of that money would be profit.

I remember sitting in the client's workroom with their project team when the budget holder/purchaser/head of the show popped her head in the room with "yet one more needed enhancement" followed by the $1.4 million dollar reminder.

I did the most nerve-wracking thing I had done since starting at the company. I looked at the project manager as his boss walked away and said, "Look, you paid $1.4 million for what we have to offer and she keeps wanting to change that. We need to maximize what you can do with what you bought before we derail everything. Do you want to tell her or do you want me? You are going to have to use what you bought or pay for these additional requests."

He agreed to talk with her. He did and I have never heard those words again. They became raving fans, offering referrals and speaking at conferences with us. They paid more for additional services as they grew into them. I learned that the customer wasn't always right.

Boundaries and guide rails were important and pushback was possible.

And sometimes you just have to fire them

I like to use this analogy from my husband, Frank (it's not just his name, it's his adjective). Frank has owned his landscaping business for over 25 years. With only word-of-mouth advertising and high-end clientele, he stakes his business on his reputation.

About six years in, Mrs. Chautauqua (name changed to protect the guilty) called and said she would be having a Fourth of July party the next weekend and she needed Frank to come burn their brush pile. He explained that due to heat and drought, there was a burn ban in place. She said again (louder) that she was having guests and didn't want to see the pile and he needed to come and burn it. He said again that it was a fire hazard for both the woods and her house and it could cost him his company. He repeated that the state had a burn ban and he wouldn't do that.

She replied with, "Let me put *Doctor* Chautauqua on the phone."

He said, "You can put *Emperor* Chautauqua on the phone for all I care. If he doesn't have the power to revoke the governor's burn ban, then it's not going to happen."

That was the first time Frank fired a client. I listened to that call while holding our first baby, having just quit my job to be a stay-at-home mom. Could we have used the money? Of course. But doing the wrong thing is never right.

MSPs have to decide where their boundaries are when it comes to their product/tool stack. The Customer Success Manager must stick to it. It is better to fire one bad customer than to potentially "light a fire" inside the business.

Doing the wrong thing is never right

Now if you are tempted to fire every third customer, there is undoubtedly a different problem that needs to be addressed first. That is a topic for another time. The critical point here is that MSPs are experts in helping business owners secure, support, and scale technology to achieve business goals. Alignment to the preferred tech stack helps do this efficiently and cost effectively. Note: "Tech stack" refers to the preferred products/services that an MSP delivers.

As we wrap up why Customer Success is important, we will take a quick look at the possibilities if we can get it right.

12-Star Customer Success program

Let's take a detour from the land of challenges and common sense and enter the realm of make-believe. I was interviewing for a VP of Customer Success position for an ed tech company. Round one went well so I was assigned a performance task. I was asked to design a 12-star Customer Success program. I had heard of 5-star programs before, but they wanted me to imagine a program that was beyond the realm of the real world. I was not bound by any of the normal restrictions of time, travel, or budget.

NEED SOME HELP WITH THE WHY?

Check out:

Creating Magic: 10 Common Sense Leadership Strategies from a Life at Disney

Lee Cockrell

This follows the theory that if you shoot for the moon and miss, you will land among the stars (Norman Vincent Peale). If I could present a compelling vision of a 12-star program, then it could contain all of the elements of a more realistic 5-star program.

It was undoubtedly my favorite interview task ever. They wanted over-the-top and I went there. As the company was in ed tech, their customers were school systems who frequently were training on technology and other topics in Professional

Learning Communities (PLCs). In this 12-star program, we did our training at a tropical resort known as a PL-Sea.

With personalized instruction, custom technology toolkits, and white glove training, the resort provided customized training, aligned to each school systems' needs. Sentiment ran high. Stress was eliminated. Tickets were resolved like magic. You get the idea. I emailed my 12-star proposal. That afternoon, a former boss offered me a position I couldn't refuse. I followed up my proposal email with a note to let the 12-star company know that I was no longer interested in the job and headed to New York to onboard for my new position.

It didn't end there. The ed tech company called me back. They asked if I would meet with some of their executive team even though I wasn't interested in the position. They were hoping I was willing to talk through how I came up with the 12-star program, and more important, what my vision was to convert it to a 5-star time- and budget-bound program.

> *Understanding "the why" isn't enough; you also need to understand "the how"*

Their team was great. They came with lots of questions and walked away with lots of notes. This company knew the stats and had the common sense to want to build a 5-star Customer Success program. But they still didn't have a framework for how to get there—or the metrics to ensure success. By pushing their thinking out of the realm of reality it allowed them to see what they were missing.

So what would a 12-star program look like for you?

- Reports magically appear

- Every customer receives a QBR quarterly

  Although when we talk about segmentation, we are going to see that quarterly isn't for everyone, so let's say every customer receives a business review as scheduled.

- Customers are excited to come to business reviews
- Customers agree to every project recommendation
- Each business review ends with referrals

And better yet:

- You have a dashboard with instant insights

Where are our customers ...

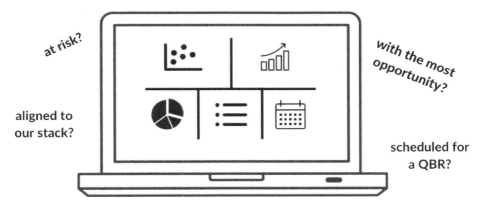

To be honest, that doesn't sound like a 12-star program (except the magic part); it sounds like a realistic 5-star program if we get all of the elements in place to make it happen.

And understanding *the why* behind CS is not enough. We need to know *the how* in order to do just that.

Are you like Paul where your own Customer Success is not scalable? Or are you aiming to operationalize your CS programs and define the components (include guide rails for your clients)? Do you want to automate metrics so you have insights for actions and next steps? Either way, we will walk through the options as we consider the 3Ps: People, Process and Product for successful CS.

If you still haven't bought into the power of CS and need some help with the why, I recommend you read *Creating Magic: 10 Common Sense Leadership Strategies from a Life at Disney* by Lee Cockrell. It is based on the teachings at the world-renowned Disney Institute. (Then have a team brainstorming session around creating your own 5-minute magic.)

If you believe Customer Success needs to be a focus, make a commitment. As in everything, you don't do it all at once. Take notes. Prioritize. Set a goal. Take action. Let's dive in!

Takeaways

- Relying on the instinct of MSP owners can't be your CS program. If you want to grow, you need a process that is independent of any person

- Don't try to automate the entire human element

- The customer is not always right

- MSPs need metrics to demonstrate their impact on their customer's business and how their customer's success may impact their own business

- The tech stack for an MSP defines their company helping them support, secure, scale their clients' businesses

- CS is an iterative process. Start with one thing and work to improve

- As you look to make an impact, consider prioritizing which of the 3Ps: People, Product, and Process that you want to address first

PART 2
THE HOW

CHAPTER 3

LET'S GET TO WORK

Remember back in the Introduction where I told you I taught high school? You are about to get a rude reminder as I ask you to take out your notebook and tell you *there will be a test*. Don't panic, I rarely assign detention and I am confident that you will pass this test.

In this section, The How, we are going to first talk about the three areas that impact a Customer Success program. They are *People*, *Process*, and *Product*. We will take a quick look at what happens if one of these components is missing and then take a deeper dive into actions you can take to increase the impact of each area. As we take that deep dive, we have worksheets that will help you document the steps you need to take along the way to define (or refine) your own Customer Success program.

Let me make that easy for you. Download the workbook at:

lifecycleinsights.io/literally

We will be needing that shortly.

The 3 Ps

Regardless of where you are in your journey to a 5-star or 12-star Customer Success program, continuous improvement is key. Companies, departments, and programs have unique strengths and weaknesses. By identifying and prioritizing areas of weakness, you can work to improve one bit at a time.

Whether you are just starting to look at Customer Success as an area of focus or are ready to automate your Customer Success insights, this section will outline potential next steps.

Consider these three specific areas to triage and decide where you want to focus first.

People/Program

Whether CS is one of many roles you perform in the company or a dedicated position, having time focused on the health and success of your customer is vital.

Process

The number one thing any company can do to improve customer health is to transition Customer Success efforts from *reactive* to *proactive* and document what that looks like.

Product

Last, those products need to be "as automated as possible" to provide the company actionable insights and next steps in the human element and customer engagement.

There is power in these Ps! If you get them all right, the power turns into success.

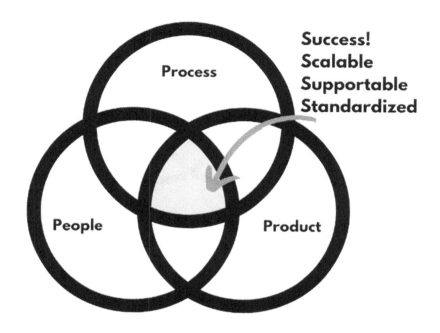

The missing link—where People, Process, and Product overlap

Let's talk about what it looks like when we have a weakness in one of these areas. It is very possible that you are reading this because you have great Customer Success folks or are a great one yourself and want to scale. Even if the process is undefined and undocumented (or poorly documented), it is likely that you have some process in place. So let's look at the overlap where there are good people and processes but no product.

This can lead to symptoms of low achievement, no accountability, and no metrics to track (or at least not easily).

There are so many sayings that point to why this is a problem.

"What is inspected is what is expected"

—attributed to W. Edwards Deming, among others

Sales teams have tools to track leads generated, conversion rates, and quotas met. Support teams have tools to track ticket close rates, escalations, and Customer Satisfaction scores (CSAT). Customer Success "borrows" metrics from sales products in terms of renewals and retention rates. They attribute some portion of the support CSAT or Net Promoter scores (NPS) to Customer Success. By cobbling together metrics from other teams and other tools, it is easy to see how there is little accountability directly associated with their work.

If everything is automated, a "success" review feels more like an autopsy than a wellness checkup

If it is a challenge to "inspect" the work due to tracking across multiple systems, it is no surprise that achievement and results are lacking. The need for a single solution is well-known. UserIQ, a CS platform for software (SaaS) companies, states that "only 25% of Customer Success teams use a single consolidated tool and 64% have plans to simplify their technology stack."

If we tie this back into our conversation on squishy metrics, it is obvious where a tool to track these metrics could impact our own success with customers. If CSMs had a single product to align their metrics and insights with their processes, imagine how much more effective they could be.

We will dive in deeply in Chapter 10. But for now, the question to ask is, where do CSMs go for managing their work in terms of:

- Customer health
- Identifying opportunities
- Managing the process
  (goals, tasks, communications,
  QBRs/business reviews)
- Getting insights into which actions to take next

The missing link: People

One thing that is not a secret is that MSPs are highly focused on products and process... "If you have to do something twice, automate it," as my business partner reminds us.

Because technology is a passion, we often hear our prospects share their CS process and product like this:

> "We have automation in place to track ticket close rates and collect CSAT info. We get metrics from our outsourced help desk, and I get additional data from my techs. I get customer feedback when I meet with them for their renewal."

Sound familiar? There are two main issues with this. First, for you as the MSP, this is too late! Completely reactive with no prior insight to potential churn. Second, for your customer, it feels robotic and automated and not like a way of building a relationship. In this case, a review of their "success" feels more like an autopsy than a wellness check-up.

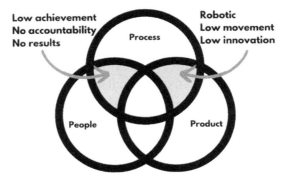

That is what happens when process and product overlap without a CS program that allows for some focus on this work. If someone (or someones) are not innovating around success, it will continue to be reactive.

The missing link: Process

I saved this overlap for last because I think it will resonate most. What happens when you have people and products but are lacking process? This feels like:

- Uncertainty
- Inconsistency
- Chaos

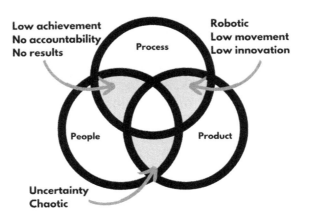

Like Paul, our MSP owner from earlier, with no process in place, the chaos-induced anxiety is often paralyzing or leads to burnout. We hear the refrain "too busy working *in* the business to work *on* the business."

Without process, every escalation feels like a fire. Little issues become big issues because no one saw them coming. Silence from a client is deadly. That is a client that gets swept away by a competitor.

> "For every customer who complains there are 26 customers who don't say anything. Instead of vocalizing their frustrations to your support team, they simply stop buying from you and cancel their subscription." —Fred Reichheld, Bain & Company

Overlap FTW

On the happier end of the spectrum, you need a process in place to capitalize on your raving fans. There should be a repeatable process for getting testimonials, referrals and upsells. Imagine the work you are missing by not having a process for this. (Are you taking notes? Did you write that down?)

So what happens when you get it right and hit the target where people, product, and process overlap? Success! Better yet, it is success for both you and for your customers. That success helps everyone's business grow as it is scalable, supportable, and standardized.

The Secret

Align your success with their success. Businesses that measure success based on impact for their customers beat out those only measuring dollars.

We are about to dive into the details. But first, your test. Which of these areas should be your focus?

Takeaways

> - It is important to consider your CS program in terms of people, product, and process
> - Choosing one area of focus is how continuous improvement begins
> - If your program has a weakness in the area of *People*, the symptoms are low motivation and or robotic interactions
> - If your program has a weakness in the area of *Process*, the symptoms are feelings of uncertainty or chaos
> - If your program has a weakness in the area of *Product*, the symptoms are a lack of accountability and/or results

CHAPTER 4

PEOPLE

Now that we have identified the target, let's look at each of the P's individually. A word of caution: When everything is a priority, nothing is. Decide what's most critical and let's tackle it one item at a time. We will start with *People*.

Even though people buy products from companies, in reality, people do business with people. Had I been able to buy my minivan online, like I could today, I would have. So how do MSPs find a balance between selling technology and selling success for their customers as strategic partners? It requires a human element.

On a "Business of Tech" podcast by Dave Sobel, he drew attention to this very scenario around commoditization in the space. He posed the question that if you can buy a car online, why can't you buy managed services online? I would claim that no matter how you side with Dave, it only points to a stronger need for a focus on your Customer Success program.

Let's say you agree with the notion that businesses could buy your managed services online. How would you know the health of that customer's account? Are the usual metrics—tickets, CSAT, NPS scores—enough? Would you wait until they clicked a button to cancel and fire up a rescue mission? Those are all reactive.

What would you need to do to see if your services are helping them achieve their business goals? We recall from earlier the statistic saying this is the driver for businesses buying services—76% of customers expect businesses they buy from to understand their needs. What would that look like?

- QBRs (or business reviews)

- Touch point calls

- Surveys (for those smaller contracts where some personalized automation would do)

These are all human engagements. To maximize their value, the role of Customer Success (whether part or all of someone's responsibility) should be to track and identify proactive health metrics such as sentiment or leadership buy-in so action can be taken before a click to cancel.

Now, let's take the alternate position on Dave Sobel's question. If you disagree that your managed services could not be purchased online, then you have already argued the point. Your services provide a human element right from the start. Customer Success is an addition or expansion of that human element that cements a relationship. And with the trend of commoditization in the MSP space, those who excel at the human element are the ones that will win—not only new customers, but staving off lower-priced competitors from poaching existing business.

When software sales started transitioning from one-time licenses to subscription models, the acronym SaaS, for Software as a Service, became the standard. As the products and services of MSPs became all-you-can-eat packages based on recurring revenue, the MSP's focus moved from strictly supporting technology to a service that aids businesses to grow and be successful with the help of technology. I occasionally see the reference to this as CSaaS—Customer Success as a Service. I really believe that is what MSPs are selling to their customers... success.

While this section is titled *People*, we are really looking at optimizing the value of the human-to-human interactions that MSPs deliver daily.

We have already talked about the symptoms of what happens if your company is missing the human element—it feels robotic and impersonal and is completely reactive. Let's take a look at some of the outcomes the role should achieve.

It's time to optimize the value of human-to-human interactions that MSPs deliver daily

We will start with the responsibilities that team members who focus on Customer Success deliver. Think about where these responsibilities fall within your company:

- Help customers understand risk and exposure created by being out of alignment with industry and MSP specific best practices

- Help customers identify and manage the business impact of such risk and exposure

- Generate client-facing budgets that reflect the total cost of ownership (TCO) of the customer's entire technology fleet, including those not managed by the MSP

- Responsible for client retention and success (track escalations, CSAT, NPS, etc.)

- Carry a quota or KPI attached to renewals or full stack adoption

- Proficient in regulatory compliance as it pertains to not only technology but also people and process

- Cultivate referral relationships

You might see that these duties span departments in your MSP, or as a sole-owner, you are doing them all. Customer Success is a cross-functional role in that it connects the work of many departments. It is evident in that list where sales is involved. Support and techs who drive the work through tickets are present. Account management and C-Suite conversations at the vCIO level are also brought to light.

If you are thinking about what this looks like in your MSP and you have named four different humans, consider how it plays out. Does it feel siloed? Or is it a well-oiled machine with strong communication both internally and externally? The role of Customer Success is often as the connector both within various departments across the organization as well as in strategic relationship with your customers.

I asked experienced sales and support leaders to chime in on this. Here are their thoughts:

From Sales

> "So you may ask why sales cares or has a say in client success. Our success in new and existing client growth goes hand in hand with the client's success. Sales and client success aren't silos. When sales and CS are aligned, it generates the energy to build what really creates customer success: strong relationships, and that leads to referrals."
>
> —Sean Lardo, VP Partner Development
> lifelong advocate of relationship selling

From Support

> "I have often seen people confuse and/or morph the roles and responsibilities of Customer Success vs. Customer Support. Both groups have a significant impact on your brand and are obviously critical to your operations. One major difference, however, is that Customer Support is very reactive, and ticket resolution metrics do not build and sustain customer loyalty. Conversely, Customer Success is proactive, and will help your customers realize the value of the investment they have made with your company. When both Customer Support and Customer Success are a priority, the result is raving fans."
>
> —Nick Coniglio, Managing Partner and Co-Founder
> Lifecycle Insights

Studies show that the human element is not just critical but, in fact, differentiates you from your competitors. MSPs are masters of process. There are processes in place for replacing switches, servers, and firewalls. Processes also need to be in place to move a CS program from reactive to proactive. That can help define (or refine) a program that scales and leads the company to success.

Takeaways

- CS is a cross-functional role

- Whether it's one person wearing three hats, three distinct teams, or somewhere in between... you must account for the three roles of Sales, Support, and Customer Success. Any gap in one of these areas puts you in a precarious position in comparison with your competitors

- Customer Success is a differentiator

- Business reviews are the foundational element

- You must start somewhere for continuous improvement

- What MSPs are really selling to their customers is *success*

- Whether it is all or part of a position in your company, a focus on CS is a baseline standard

CHAPTER 5

PROCESS DEVELOPMENT FRAMEWORK

But first, let's prove a point:

How's your memory? Let's find out. Look at the numbers below for 10 seconds. Try to memorize them.

389525912022857

Now cover them. See how many you can write down in order.

How'd you do? Psychologists say the average person can hold 7 (plus or minus 2) "chunks" of information in their active memory. So if you scored between 5 and 9, that is fairly typical. If you scored greater than 9, then maybe you knew the secret.

In my college psychology class, the professor had us stand up. He would write a string of digits on the board, count to 10, then erase them. He would then see who could recite the string. And those who could accurately remember them all remained standing. With each string, he would add another digit. Most of the class made it through 8, then we started to lose folks, quickly. After 15, I was the only one left. At 28 he stopped me with the question: How are you doing that?

My response was simple. The theory says "chunks" not digits, so I would read the numbers as football plays: "38-95-25 hike", "91-20-22 hike," etc. so that 6 digits were only taking one "chunk" in my memory.

Apologies for the side route, but it did teach us two things:

1. I am a nerd
2. Chunking information can be extremely powerful

It also prompts us to ask the question: How can we use this power to make our business more efficient?

Chunking or "segmenting" your customer base can help you deliver better and faster customer service with greater success (oh, and sales). This process will help you give every customer the attention they need, want, and deserve.

In one of my days as a customer (data/accountability coordinator), I was assigned a new CSM from one of our software vendors. I had countless other roles and responsibilities and used their product regularly with little problem. As my new CSM, he decided to set up weekly calls with me to see if I needed any help. While I appreciated the concept, I valued my time more. Plus, I was "that" customer. *Don't call me. I'll call you... and when I do, I would really rather it be via email or chat with an immediate response.*

> *Chunking your customer base can help you deliver better and faster customer service with greater success (and sales!)*

This CSM wouldn't listen, and Friday mornings at 9:00 A.M. when I didn't join the meeting, he would call my cell and then the office line. After multiple iterations of this—along with email responses to my questions that were pushed to "Friday calls"—I had him taken off our account. The company happily obliged, and I am now quite good friends with the other CSM, who I "chatted with" for about five minutes per month to get my questions answered.

That said, there are services where I very much need and want more engagement. And the first responsibility in CS is to define for each customer what level of engagement and communication cadence is appropriate and effective. If you can figure out which experience your customer wants (and needs), then you are more likely to earn raving fans.

That is the goal in segmenting your customer base. The book *Data Mining Technique in CRM* (Tsiptsis & Chorianopoulos, Wiley: 2010) defines segmentation as the process of dividing customers into distinct groups to develop differentiated communication strategies based on given variables. This allows for delivery of "personalized" yet "optimized" customer account management. It maximizes company resources by determining if clients are best served with high-touch, mid-touch or tech-touch engagement.

We are going to work on creating those segments for your client base. If you haven't already downloaded the worksheets, visit the website now, or go old school and mark up this book.

lifecycleinsights.io/literally

The first step in segmentation is to brainstorm all of the characteristics and variables that will help categorize clients. I typically like to consider variables that determine how much attention and communication they might need, or the value of each to your company.

As you brainstorm, list as many ideas as you can think of in the box on the next page. I start with some of the obvious elements like MRR and company size. Take 1-2 minutes to think through this.

Variable brainstorming list:

- MRR
- Customer size

Hopefully you have a good-sized list to work with. Here are some that I came up with. Feel free to steal any or all that seem relevant to add to your list.

Variable brainstorming list:

- MRR/ARR
- Size (#users/endpoints)
- Influence/Reference value
- New vertical
- Effort
- Opportunity
- Technology needs/dependency
- Industry/Regulatory Compliance

Now, we are going to split these variables into two categories.

Category 1: VALUE

Group all of the terms that represent the value of the customer to *your* business.

Category 2: COMPLEXITY

Group the variables that will stand for complexity or effort or the impact technology has on *your client's* business and *your* business.

Go back to the list and circle all of the variables for Category 1 and underline those for Category 2.

Now move these variables into the table below. Write your variables in the appropriate columns (ignore the scoring guide at the bottom for now).

Variable Worksheet

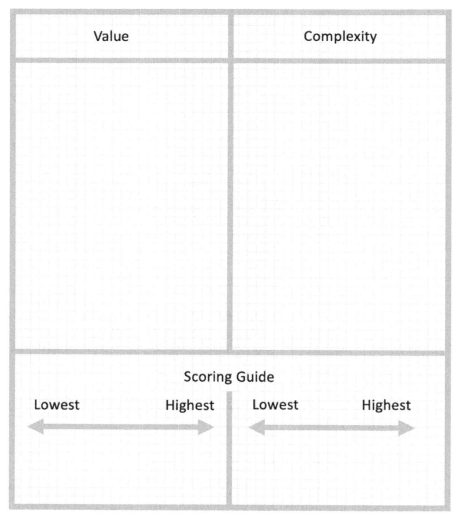

THE VARIABLES

Here is what my sheet looks like:

Value	Complexity
• MRR/ARR • Size (#users/endpoints) • Influence/Reference value • New vertical	• Effort • Opportunity • Technology needs/dependency • Industry/Regulatory Compliance

Now we are going to simplify things. We are going to choose one metric from each column that will allow you to easily assign a number for each client. For most MSPs, Monthly Recurring Revenue (MRR) is the obvious choice for value. (If you are transitioning from a break-fix shop to an MSP, then you might want to consider potential MRR or size based on the number of users or endpoints).

If you aren't sitting in front of your contracts with precise MRR values, take a first pass at this activity by assigning customers a score on a 1-100 point scales. A score of 90-100 would represent your highest paying customers and a score between 1-10 might be a client who only uses one of your services.

As you consider the variable of "Value," let's record your lowest and highest MRR values (this will go in as part of our Scoring Guide).

Pro Tip: Don't overcomplicate this. Choose the top end (what does *great* look like?) and the bottom end (what does *very bad* look like). Then add a description for middle-ground ratings.

Scoring Guide			
Lowest	Highest	Lowest	Highest
$1,500	$27,000		

Because we are going to use this information to decide how often and what types of communication our customers will receive, we need to think about setting a "cut score." A cut score is a number you set to help divide your values into ranges for easy analysis. We are looking to define what numbers separate good and medium and bad (or green, yellow, red).

- Is there a minimum threshold that customers pay where you would deliver more face-to-face (even if done virtually) meetings?

- Do you have an MRR value that you would like to set as a target for some of your smaller clients to make them more profitable?

- Is the middle number in the range a good start?

Use your answers to these questions to help define your cut score for your Value range. Enter that number in the worksheet as shown below.

Scoring Guide			
Lowest	Highest	Lowest	Highest
$1,500	$9,000	$27,000	
	Define your cut score		

Now we will work through the same process for Complexity. For the variable of Complexity, you might not have a predefined number (like dollars). So you will need to develop and define a rule for what would represent a "0" and what would represent "100. Here is one way of looking at Complexity.

Scoring Guide				
Lowest		Highest	Lowest	Highest
$1,500	$9,000	$27,000	Low compliance	High compliance
	Define your cut score			

If you are the only person assigning numbers (for now), this might be enough in terms of details. However, we are aiming to scale, so provide enough detail that you could eventually hand this task to someone else. (Are you starting to feel that work-life balance tip in your favor?) If you have an entire team, make sure the rules for scoring are clear. These rules should be a clear guide on how to score a client on a single element or variable based on levels. Add details or examples as needed to clarify the levels as you document this.

This is the exciting part. We are going to put it into action. Now we test our metrics with a handful of customers. This way we can adjust before going through our entire customer base.

Now that you have defined your metrics, go to the second worksheet on the following page.

List 5 customers in the left hand column and enter numbers in their Value and Complexity columns based on the rules you just defined.

Customer Segments

Customer	Value	Complexity

Pro Tip:

Do not use 5 of the "same" types of customers for this activity. Use one of your largest customers, one of your relatively small customers and a few in between. That was easy!

Customer	Value	Complexity	Segment
• Creative Designs	$18,000	85	
• GetWell Medical Services	$7,250	95	
• Home Inspection Inc	$1,900	15	
• Hunter Lodge	$2,210	25	
• People R Us	$4,000	75	

Now, let's start building a visual to help us understand the value and needs of our customers. You will be working with the table we just built and the Variable Worksheet at the same time. You can see that Value runs across the horizontal axis and Complexity up the vertical axis. Start adding coordinates to represent your customers as shown here:

There are many variations of how to look at each quadrant. Here is a quick idea of what you might be thinking about each area:

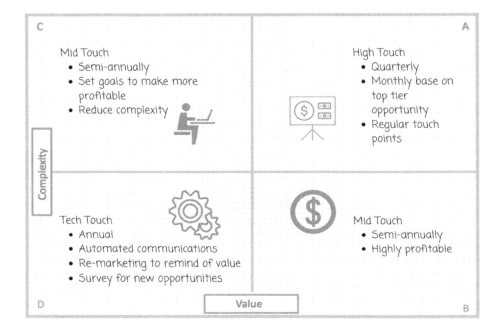

After seeing that, are the right companies landing in the right quadrants based on your measures? If not, now is the time to make adjustments to your rules and definitions around the metrics.

Once you have it set, you should fill it out for your entire customer base. If you have a dozen clients, then plotting them manually on this graph is a good start.

But again, we are trying to scale, so if it is time to break out the spreadsheet, head back to our Resource Page where we have built a spreadsheet for you.

lifecycleinsights.io/literally

As we review each quadrant, we want to consider what the best customer experience would be for each segment. We will outline this further in Chapter 8, but for just a taste, consider business reviews.

First, we should address the elephant in the room (or an entire pack of smaller elephants): the naming of the business review. We hear:

The worst name (QBR) is probably the most popular, but they are often *not* done quarterly, and we just agreed that maybe everyone doesn't warrant one quarterly. So for the sake of argument, let's say the Q stands for *Quality* and run with QBR (as *Quality Business Review*) since that is what the industry already knows.

From a business process perspective, many companies want to get all of their clients into the same communication cycle. The power of process is that fewer items fall through the cracks, and new team members and new clients can easily understand the expectations.

We have just segmented our clients and it is quite clear that each segment has a different priority level in terms of value and need. When I had the CSM removed from my account as a customer, it was because the cadence of communication was overkill and provided no value. I found it frustrating. We don't want to frustrate our clients. So as we look at each segment, really think about how often a client should meet with you.

You should be able to provide value, address risk, and provide strategic guidance in regard to technology. A small construction business will have a very different need than a high-compliance defense contractor. There is no set framework in the MSP space, but here are a few methods proposed by some industry experts.

- Alex Rogers at Chartec recommends an SBR meeting cadence based on MRR. For every $1000 in MRR a client spends, they should get that many business reviews within a year. A $4k MRR client would then have a true QBR done quarterly.

- Nigel Moore of the Tech Tribe recommends a frequent cadence—at least quarterly. More often, he believes MSPs should meet monthly until clients are fully aligned to your stack.

In high school, my English teacher was asked how long an essay should be. She responded with the answer often attributed to Winston Churchill in regard to length of speeches: "As long as a woman's skirt: short enough to keep attention and long enough to cover the topic." Your QBR cadence should follow the same rule. Whatever cadence provides strategic value for a segment is the right answer. The important part is to define a process and implement it. Then, adjust as you go.

We frequently tout, "Don't let perfection be the enemy of good." So let's put pen to paper and make a plan. In each segment quadrant, enter the number of "ideal" business reviews a client would have in a year. Save some space as we will add a lot more thinking here in the Process section.

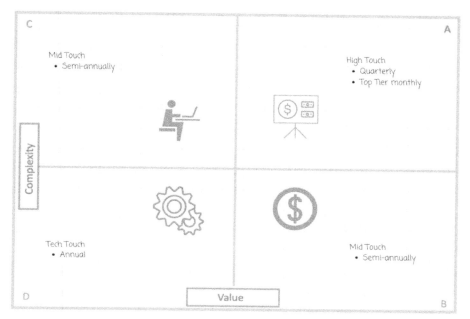

There are multiple considerations for the use of segmentation. Segmentation is mission critical when it comes to business reviews. Your Statement of Work (SOW) should outline this cadence and you must adhere to it.

It is not just important for your clients' security and risk needs to be addressed in the MSA. In the event of any breach or ransomware attack, your own cybersecurity insurance company will want to know that these QBRs have been delivered. Segmentation will also play a key role in helping CSMs deliver service faster. Building efficiencies in the Customer Success program will allow for a proactive approach as opposed to a reactive one.

Takeaways

- Segmenting your customer base gives every client the service they need, NOT the exact same service

- Segmenting your clients by their value and complexity helps you align communication best practices

- Done is better than perfect. Start somewhere.

CHAPTER 6

HEALTH

Let's think back to the blind-sided phone call our CSM, Kerrie, received in Chapter 1 when Michael, her customer, called to cancel the contract. Keep that in mind as you take a look back at your segmentation graph.

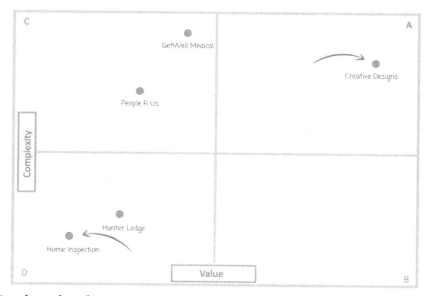

Look at the client in the top right quadrant—a high complexity but super high-value company. What if they were the one to call you today to cancel?

Did that get your heart racing? Palms sweating? Stomach churning?

Now look at the name in the bottom left quadrant—low complexity but low value. If they were the ones to make the call, how would it feel?

I know all clients matter and it wouldn't feel good, but I bet the anxiety level would not be as dramatic. The truth of it is that a complete blind-side should be very rare. But we shouldn't rely only on our gut as a way to determine whether a client might churn.

Let's think about customer health as we would think about our own physical health. There are many illnesses that can be prevented or reduced in severity with early diagnosis. Annual physicals are one component. With the advancement of fitness trackers that can monitor heart rate, glucose levels, sleep scores, and fitness stats, it is possible to see even earlier indicators of potential illness.

Proactive metrics are key in business just as in health. If a CSM starts to see warning signs of an unhappy customer, they can take action to recover the relationship. And even better, building great Customer Success practices and processes can have them working proactively in order to stay drama-free. This is the ideal state.

To define how to get there, we will start with metrics. If you have a team of CSMs, this is a great brainstorming activity to do as a group. If you haven't, get out your thinking hat/notebook/whiteboard/doodling app and the Health Score Worksheet.

lifecycleinsights.io/literally

Customer Health Worksheet

Metric	Low	High

Lifecycle Insights

Looking at the client list from your segmentation activity, circle a couple of your happiest customers. Try to select at least one from each segment. Now list how you know they are happy (these don't have to be numbers, just put down whatever comes to mind).

In our imaginary list of clients, I can tell you that Creative Designs loves us because we are always reaching out with cutting edge products in their industry. I am jotting down the metric "Adoption of stack" because if we offer it, they have it.

This is one of those situations where you must defeat the blank page to get the ideas flowing. If you are atypical, then you have a thoroughly well-documented customer health platform that includes a health score. More typically, however, you rely on your gut. We already discussed this. Your gut won't scale.

If you have struggled with some ideas, feel free to steal some from this list:

Health Metric Brainstorming

- Adoption of stack
- Engagement of leadership
- Regularly schedule and attend QBRs
- Responsive to emails
- CSAT
- NPS
- Providing referrals

Now consider your 5 unhappiest customers. How do you know they are unhappy? Write down the signs/symptoms.

If you are fighting with yourself (or me!) on this, you might be saying, "I just know!" You must ask yourself if you truly want to scale. The control freak in all of us believes we are the only ones who can relate to the customer and provide that value as a strategic partner. Been there, done that. That's why I'm here to help you see the value (and not just in dollars) of building health metrics and a process so your customers are over-whelmingly supported by an entire team. Don't worry. We will start with baby steps.

Okay, back to the worksheet. Jot down any more ideas.

Health Metric Brainstorming

- Adoption of stack
- Engagement of leadership
- Regularly schedule and attend QBRs
- Responsive to emails
- CSAT
- NPS
- Providing referrals
- Customer calls for advice
- Strong internal champion
- They have offered to give referrals

Now let's think of any negatives that might be a red flag.

Red Flag List

- Change in leadership
- Merging/acquisition talks
- Pivots in the business
- Illness
- Recent significant tech or security issue
- Repeated questions/concerns on the same unresolved issues

Now for the Wild Cards. If someone called you out of the blue to cancel, what unique reason might they have that we didn't already mention? Add those to a Red Flag List.

Are there any signs that we could have seen this coming? If so, add them to the list. One of our partners shared that a client asking for the password to the key systems was an immediate danger sign. Maybe add that to your Red Flag List.

Please don't overthink here. A minute ago we were going with your gut and now you are perseverating.[2] What is top of mind?

Okay, we should now be looking at a good-sized list. I know it was a lot of work to pull together, but next we are going to prune it. Our goal is to cut this list to the fewest number of

---

[2] *perseverating: to prolong an action far beyond what's required.*
EX: sandpapering a table until you go through the wood

metrics that will still give us an accurate health score. Unlike in segmentation, we don't need to reduce this to only two variables. Nick Mehta, CEO of Gainsight, has said that it is a common misconception that customer health can be derived from a single variable. So, let's see if we can narrow it down to a reasonable handful.

Here are some questions to consider in pruning the list:

- Does one metric actually rely on another? If so, only keep the main one.

- Do two or more metrics actually measure the same thing? Is there overlap?

- Would one of those red flags or hot buttons be enough to override an entire health score and shift it to "red?" (I put leadership change or M&A in this category.)

Now that we have a leaner list (see, we are getting healthier already!), it is time to write some rules around health.

Customer Health Worksheet

Metric	Low			High
• Sentiment	Unhappy	Questionable	Satisfied	Raving Fan
• Stack adoption	<25%	26-50%	51-75%	76-100%
• Engagement	None	Occasional	Regular	Highly
• CSAT	<25%	26-50%	51-75%	76-100%

Is there major overlap in some of the metrics? Can you eliminate any more? We are going for the fewest number of measures to get you the most accurate health score. Less is more. But in this case, it is also efficient—which means you will get a solid health score quickly and easily—saving you time and money.

Now it is time to put your metrics to the test. If you have a spreadsheet of clients from your segmentation activity, you can expand from there. If not, the Customer Health Tracker is yours for the tracking.

Customer Health Worksheet

Client	Health Metrics	Average	Health	Segment

Lifecycle Insights

List your clients down the left and the metrics across the top.

Now enter values for each metric. You can see that these metrics do not have values you can pull from a PSA or ticketing system. You will want to define rules around how to score each metric on a 100-point scale. (Are you perseverating again? Stop. Use that gut and any tool you have to get your best approximation and let's see how it goes.)

Here's my sample set:

Customer Health Worksheet

Client	Health Metrics				Average	Health	Segment
	Sentiment	CSAT	Org	Renewal			
Creative Designs	95	78	62	95			
GetWell	56	34	10	40			
Home Inspections	85	75	80	90			
Hunter Lodge	20	20	25	25			
People R Us	95	80	85	95			

Lifecycle Insights

Now let's average these scores. I told you spreadsheets have value. If you want to transfer your work to a spreadsheet, you shouldn't be surprised to learn that we have a template just for you:

lifecycleinsights.io/literally

Now review your calculations. In the screenshot below, we defined clients "healthy," "needs attention," and "at risk" based on the following cut scores:

- Red: 0-50% At risk
- Yellow: 51-75% Needs attention
- Green: 76-100% Healthy

Spot-check some customers. Look at them in order from healthiest to least healthy. Does that look right? Is it aligned with your gut? Things to consider: Do you need to change, add, or eliminate any of the metrics? Should you revise your rules? Would an adjustment to your cut scores better group your clients?

You really do want to spend some time looking over your metrics and dialing them in. Remember, the goal is to be able to quickly look at that total health score and act on it. That requires that you trust it. This might take several iterations. Again, it is all about continuous improvement.

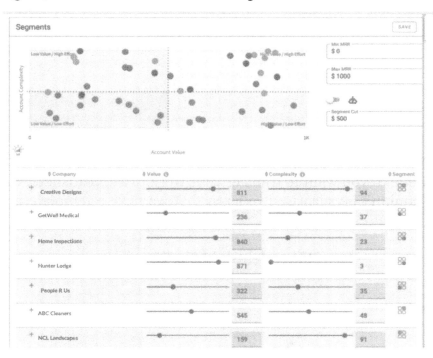

This is what I like to see happen with my segmentation quadrants and health scores. (See the full color screenshots on our resource page at http://lifecycleinsights.io/literally. Even better when the live version is actually in red, yellow, green!) So break out the colored pencils, advanced spreadsheets skills, or a CS tool that will help you get this view.

As a CSM, the very first question Kerrie should be asked at her weekly (monthly/quarterly) review is: "Which clients are at risk for churn?" That should be followed up quickly with: "What is the risk to our business? And what are we going to do about it?"

If Kerrie had completed the activity, she could respond to the first question immediately. The graph gives a hint at how to answer that second question, but she should have more information at her fingertips in terms of both risk of churn and opportunity of upsells.

In the next chapter we will talk more about the metrics Kerrie would need to understand the financial risks and upsell potential.

Takeaways

- A customer health score lets you be proactive

- Clearly defining health rules is important in order for them to be effective (i.e., provide insights that can lead to action)

- Regular health checkups in business are as important as health checkups for people

- Develop plans for customers that have lower health scores to mitigate your risk

- Don't ignore customers with high health scores—focus on keeping them at that level!

CHAPTER 7

OPPORTUNITY

For MSPs, there are as many unique ways to position and sell your services as there are MSPs. I will categorize some of the most popular methods and strategies we hear from our partners at Lifecycle Insights. We are talking about opportunities to sell into existing client space. If you are not native to sales-speak, this is called "white space." One popular phrase is "land and expand." This is where you sell a smaller product or service to a customer, and then (thanks to your incredible Customer Success) they expand into your other offerings.

Since we just finished talking about health, there is a metric that is both an indicator of health and provides insight into opportunity. That is the notion of *stack alignment*. An MSP's product/tool stack is really the DNA of their business. It includes all the tools they trust, understand, support, and troubleshoot. Therefore, clients who are "all-in" in utilizing your business' complete stack are most easily supported. Not only that, but as they grow, your services are scalable and most completely secured. This is good for your client and most profitable for you. So the most important health *and* opportunity metric is stack alignment.

> *Stack alignment is the most important health and opportunity metric for the profitability of your business*

We addressed the health portion in the last chapter so now let's look at it in terms of opportunity. If you do not have a full

73

list of your tech stack, that is the place to start. Having this list will provide you quick insights into which of your clients are fully, partially, or barely aligned. You might find a service that is underutilized across your client base. Or you might find that a client that is requiring a great deal of support time from your team would be better served if they were more aligned with the technology your team is most familiar with.

Stack Builder

	Solution	Product	Vendor
1	Firewall		
2	Switching		
3	Wireless		
4	Intrusion Detection and Prevention		
5	Email Hosting		
6	Email Encryption		
7	Email Archiving		
8	Email Protection/Filtering		
9	Email Signature Management		
10	DNS Content Filtering		
11	Cloud Filter Services (SharePoint/Anchor...)		
12	Cloud Services Backup (MS365/Google)		
13	Antivirus (Traditional)		
14	Antimalware (NextGen)		
15	Cybersecurity (Managed Soc)		
16	Zero Trust		
17	Privileged Access Management (PAM)		
18	Workstation/Server Encryption		
19	Backup & Disaster Recovery		
20	Endpoint/Workstation Backup		
21	Data Loss Prevention (DLP)		
22	Mobile Device Encryption		
23	Cloud Directory Services		
24	VPN/Remote Access		
25	Multi-factor Authentication		
26	Password Manager		
27	Secure Scan/Fax		
28	SIEM/Event Log Monitoring		

	Solution	Product	Vendor
29	Third Party Audit/Pen Testing		
30	Dark Web Monitoring		
31	Social Engineering/Phishing		
32	Employee Cyber Training		
33	VOIP		
34	Print Management		
35	Website Hosting/Management		
36	Vendor Risk Management		
37	Internet Service Provider		
38	Redundant Internet		

By associating default costs for each product in your stack, you will get even more insights into the value of that opportunity.

This can provide a quick projection or forecast of the opportunities:

- Overall
- By client
- By product

Now, when Kerrie receives the question about how much the red client could cost the business, she has an easy answer.

But it gets better. When you have a view into opportunity data, your potential for growth increases (i.e., "You miss 100% of the targets you don't aim for.")

In 2020, Datto published a report on the state of MSPs and they made two compelling statements around MSP growth. They found that MSPs more than doubled their growth from their peers if they focused on:

1. Increasing their percentage of sales that were MRR (as opposed to project/break-fix work)

2. Setting growth goals
   (financial targets/quotas for their own company)

A CSM approaches a client as an advocate and trusted advisor for their clients. When seen as a trusted partner, clients are much more likely to take guidance about what technologies they need next to grow their business, as opposed to someone who is just there to sell a tool. That relationship approach is better for everyone. Clients that fully adopt your tech stack are much stickier (good for you) and get much more value (good for them). Investing in the full stack *and* the partnership required to deliver and understand the full value dramatically increases retention rates and lowers churn potential.

We mentioned earlier that if this focus on Customer Success and stack adoption/alignment is not yet a mature process in an MSP, then there is about 30% of the value of the contracts left on the table. Unlike selling to a new customer, selling within your client base is much less expensive.

Clearly identifying opportunity is the first step. Defining the process for upsells (and all other CS functions, for that matter) is next.

Takeaways

- Stack alignment is the principal overlap between customer health and opportunity
- Stack alignment insights are a great internal sales tool
- Not only does improving these opportunity metrics increase MRR but it improves client retention and satisfaction

CHAPTER 8

PROCESS

The phone rings. "Hi, Kerrie!"

"Hi, Pam!" Pam is the owner of an insurance company and a client of Kerrie's. "I put in a support ticket yesterday and I wanted to see if you would follow up on it for me."

"Absolutely! I'm glad you called. While I have you, I wanted to schedule your next business review. When might be a good day/time for you?"

MSPs tell us the responses to this vary. Which of these sounds most familiar to you:

    A. I don't really have time for that.
    B. We didn't get much value last time.
    C. What benefit will we get from this meeting?
    D. Great! We have some new business updates we want to discuss.

But what they really meant was:

    A. Ugh. Boring—No value.
    B. Waste of time.
    C. You just want to sell me something.
    D. Of course, we value this strategic conversation! You are part of our team!

Ahh... business reviews, the pillar of the Customer Success relationship between an MSP and their clients.

By *pillar,* I mean a few things:

1. Business reviews are a must do

2. Most MSPs do some kind of review even if the process is not clearly defined or adhered to

3. If you have no other component of a Customer Success program, you must start here as part of your annual renewal/review process

When it comes to doing business reviews, MSPs run the gamut from: We don't do them. We do them irregularly and inconsistently. We do them but it is very manual and time consuming. *or* We schedule ours regularly and they are automated, scalable, and efficient!

If you can't confidently say that you are at the top of your game when it comes to QBRs, then have your pen and paper ready. We have work to do! (And remember what we just learned— big potential for upsells follow this work.)

We will address other work for the Customer Success team in the following chapters, but we know that QBRs are the place to start and have the greatest impact both short and long term.

> *A strong Customer Success program is proactive. Playing whack-a-mole is not.*

Now that we have segmented our customer base, we have a good understanding of the type of client that falls into each quadrant. We are now going to start defining the processes and cadence of communication for each segment.

The key to defining a strong Customer Success program is to plan for it to be proactive. Playing whack-a-mole is not proactive. Hitting a target is. Here are some guidelines in setting those targets.

We will start by zooming into our top right quadrant. These are clients who bring the most value (MRR) to your business and have the highest needs/complexity.

For the sake of this example, we will reference one of our MSP owner Paul's largest clients—Meetme Corporation. Their MSA contract is approximately $27k per month. They have some government defense contracts and, therefore, have high security/compliance (i.e., complexity) needs.

The renewal date for their contract is March 15th. So the most important thing Paul's team needs to know is that they will have a business review 30-60 days before March 15th *and* this customer will become a raving fan by the end of that meeting. (And, yes, we have a recovery plan we will talk about later in the event that this is not the case.)

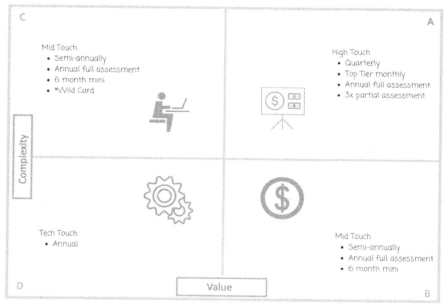

NOTE: The Wild Card. Each quarter, Paul prioritizes one client in the top left quadrant to do a full QBR in order to increase their MRR as these are his least profitable clients.

One-off meetings aren't scheduled but Paul does have checklists/processes in place defining when these may need to happen. These and all of the meetings are documented so that notes can be reviewed to help set future goals and next steps.

Business reviews help to:

- Build the relationship
- Learn or update understanding of the client's business
- Upsell
- Gauge customer health
- Set goals and define next steps

So let's dive in deep to the best practices around QBRs.

The QBR

As we started the last chapter, Kerrie was aiming to schedule a QBR with Pam, the owner of an insurance company. Fortunately, the leadership at Kerrie's MSP saw the light in terms of the value of a strong CS program, and they now have the QBRs dialed in. So Pam responded that she and her exec team were looking forward to the next QBR and could see her in three weeks. Kerrie hopped into action as three weeks was the perfect timing.

ProTip: The next QBR should actually be scheduled at the close of the previous QBR. So Kerrie still has some process improvements to make.

Before we dive into the QBR itself (including preparation and execution), let's look at a few more common conversations we have with MSPs.

Before delivering *Quality* Business Reviews, MSPs sometimes heard:

- "These business reviews are just sales calls."
- "This meeting could have been an email."
- "It didn't deliver value."

WHAT'S "JUST RIGHT?"

Check out:

The Checklist Manifesto: How to Get Things Right

Atul Gawande

The author dramatically improved surgery outcomes by standardizing and implementing a basic, but critical, checklist.

MSPs themselves would sometimes say:

"They take too long to prep."

"I don't know what to say."

If any of that sounds familiar, then we have some resources for you. And it all starts with... a process.

Processes range in format and scope. For Customer Success programs, they are often documented as either checklists or playbooks. In terms of scope, there is the bite-sized version: Prep, Review, Deliver, Reflect framework. There is also the highly-detailed document outlining every decision point along the way. We, however, will take the "Goldilocks" (just right) approach outlined in *The Checklist Manifesto* by Atul Gawande (Picador: 2010).

One of our partners, Kevin Elsing from ELBO Computing, has a process in place to run his QBRs (which he calls SBRs—Strategic Business Reviews). He uses a checklist and has given us permission to share it with you. Here is the high-level outline. To drill into each of the categories, go to our resources page and download the full checklist.

lifecycleinsights.io/literally

81

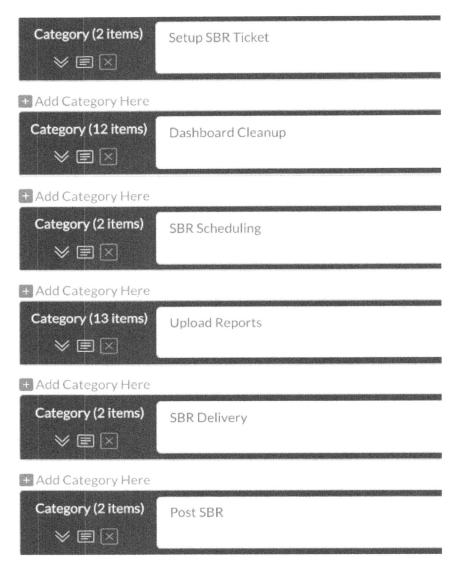

Check out our resource page for the full details
and expanded checklist: lifecycleinsights.io/literally

This checklist is very specific to his process, but in interviewing Kevin about how this checklist has changed his business, he had this to say:

> "Now that we have documented steps and Lifecycle Insights as a one-stop-shop for our vCIO process, it has personally saved me hours of prep. My intern and tech do all of the prep work and I review the document for 15 minutes before the meeting and spend about 15 minutes after the meeting to make sure all of the follow-up items have been assigned. I used to do three QBRs a week and now I can easily do three a day."

Kevin's checklist outlines his process for prepping for the business review. Now let's take a look at what MSPs should be delivering in a QBR itself.

Components of a Strategic QBR

It's been about two decades since the transformation of the IT Support industry into the Managed Service industry we know today. Along the way, specialized software platforms arrived on the scene that would promise to automate everything from software deployment and patch management to time tracking and billing. As IT companies deployed these applications and migrated to remote support and flat-rate billing plans, the best in class Managed Service Providers began to share their best practices and KPIs.

It wasn't long before thought leaders made bold statements like, "MSPs should be able to solve for at least 85% of tickets without rolling a truck" and that "automation could replace an engineer." Before long, these became foundations of the MSP industry, and of their service offerings. As MSPs went onsite less, relationships with clients suffered—and the QBR was born. As MSPs were told that they should track the amount of time that we saved with automation and review that and other KPIs with clients at regular business reviews, thus justifying their existence.

The talking points for the average QBR looked something like this:

- We automated 123 minutes of work.
- We blocked xxx spam emails.
- We caught yyy suspicious files before they could be executed.
- We solved zzz tickets.
- We completed a project on time.
- And we got great CSAT scores.
- This is why you pay us $$$$.
- Oh, and we need more money to [replace hardware / subscribe to SaaS solution / buy new shiny thing / raise MSP rates]

The problem... these are all the things your clients *expected* you to do! So the QBR quickly became a low-value, high-cost event (to your customer). How many of you want to sit through a 60-90 minute meeting, with the most expensive members of your staff, just to review KPIs you don't care about, woven into acronyms you don't understand... and end the meeting getting hit up to spend more money? *Exactly.*

What we want to share with you are some of the QBR components that hundreds of Lifecycle Insights MSP partners are currently using to be successful in painting that long-term, strategic picture with their partners. These are business reviews their customers appreciate and look forward to attending.

Agenda

This first component is the one that really sets the table for the client meeting. The agenda not only tells the customer that you are coming to have a serious, business-focused conversation, but also that your conversation will be aligned with their desired outcomes. We achieve that by sending over an agenda along with several questions asking the client about the state of their industry, their plans, and their internal stretch goals. By aligning our technology strategy with their desired business outcomes, we increase client interest in the meeting and the likelihood that they will be onboard with addressing any shortfalls we identify as standing in the way. In this manner, the agenda literally sets the stage for client engagement during the entire rest of the process.

Pro Tip: If you are a CSM and are bringing your executive leadership to the QBR, have a prep call so everyone knows their roles and company goals. Check out a sample agenda template on the resources page at:

lifecycleinsights.io/literally

Risk Assessment

When exploring the customer journey, we often discuss that while every prospect or customer starts in a different place, they often walk a similar journey. The risk assessment points out in black and white (and some red, yellow, and green) just where in the journey each customer is starting. At the end of the day, we don't have a choice but to start where we are and strategize how to improve through small, tactical adjustments in the way of recommendations.

Budget(s)

Okay, so we have our client engaged, and we know where we are... mostly. Unfortunately for our customers, technology is expensive. The budget is an important weapon at our disposal to ensure that we never have to blind-side our customer. Our MSP tools keep inventories of our client's technology assets, and we, as the MSP, can present those with end-of-life dates and costs in the form of a budget. We can even add expenses for contracts, software subscriptions, and project work to give our clients the total cost of ownership (TCO) for their technology. Now we not only know where we are, but how much it costs to maintain what we own!

Imagine telling a client 2-3 years in advance about every significant technology purchase their organization was going to make. There is no room for hurt feelings or broken trust because we know from the date we purchase an asset what it's approximate lifespan will be and we can plan for its replacement. This is strategic budgeting.

But why the above reference to multiple budget(s)? Because a near-term (6, 12, or 18-month) tactical budget can also be helpful in aiding smaller clients' decision-making processes. If a huge mega-budget that shows 5 years of expenses would seem overwhelming to your client, then presenting the budget two ways can help them digest that the big scary number is just for awareness—their IT expenses didn't go through the roof just because we took the blinders off and showed the expenses to them. A 6-month budget can often appear much more manageable and help reduce the chances of a less operationally mature client's rejection of budgeting altogether. (Yes, that can happen.)

Raj's Perspective

"I always knew the value of presenting a full budget to my clients. My previous process involved over 12 hours of spreadsheets and sweat to deliver a total cost of ownership. I would only deliver a business review once a year even for my most valuable client because of the amount of prep time. Now that it is automated, my prep time is down to one and a half hours."

Recommendations & Remediation Plan

We know the TCO of our current technology, but how much more is it going to cost to adopt the technology required to meet the business goals of our client? Maybe they are opening a new location... or maybe they are adding staff to support a new product line... or maybe the client works in a highly regulated industry and they are aligning with compliance obligations. Whatever the reason, projects happen, and their associated costs are one of the few things that may be difficult to plan for in the budget. Projects can be very profitable for MSPs, but if they aren't presented well, they can also become a bone of contention between the client and the MSP due to their occasionally reactive nature. It's important that we face projects and their associated expenses head-on and have clear expectations when setting conversations with our clients.

Ron's Story

One of Lifecycle Insights' partners, Ron, recently called us, saying he hit a problem when presenting his assessment and related projects at a QBR. As he explained, everything went well with the presentation, and the customer was engaged. He reviewed the assessment and recommended more projects than he ever thought the client would accept, just hoping they would pick some portion of the work and commit to it. When he got done presenting, he asked the client how they wanted to move forward and was stopped in his tracks when they answered, "Looks good—let's do it." It took a little back and forth before he realized they meant, "Let's do all of it." It turned out to be one of the biggest project sales he had ever closed, and provided a huge confidence boost to this MSP owner who had been struggling to scale his business.

Presentation matters, and many customers will bite off more than you anticipate if you simply go to the meeting prepared to ask, with documentation that backs up your ask. In short, plan ahead, know your goals for the meeting, and make sure your documentation supports that goal.

Executive Summary

You're busy in this new Zoom meeting world. Guess what... so are your customers. You asked them to plan 90 minutes to spend with you for a strategic meeting, but after you leave, they will sit through two more meetings, take a client to lunch, and then have an additional two meetings before checking a handful of emails and rushing the kids off to baseball practice.

The next time they think about your meeting and their technology needs may be a week later. If you successfully present your long-term strategic plan to your client at your meeting, then an Executive Summary should be designed to distill that plan down to only the things that matter in the very near future. When they look at it again in a week, it should reinforce the confidence and positivity they felt during the meeting that you could help them achieve their company goals, and make clear to them what needs to happen in the next 90-180 days to keep those goals on track.

This should be 1-page document, "reduced to ridiculous" with just enough information to keep what is important in the moment at the front and center of your client's mind. A good Executive Summary is an art form. It's hard. But when you deliver, it can be the icing on a really amazing cake.

This isn't to say that you will never bring tactical reports for supporting evidence to your strategic discussions. In fact, you'll often need actionable data to back up your forward looking strategic recommendations. Some tactical items may be included—but they will not take center stage.

- Asset List
- User List
- Contracts

- Technical docs and stats—scorecard only
  (backups, spam, malware, etc.)

I strongly suggest keeping the use of those documents to the bare minimum and letting your strategic documents run the meeting.

QBRs provide much more value than any upsells made. (And there is certainly great value in that!) QBRs are the foundation of a strategic relationship. They are forward looking. A leading industry thought leader around the impact of CS and QBRs, Gainsight, shared research confirming that business reviews provide additional insights into the sentiment and health of the client which improves retention rates along with MRR.

As we wrap up our discussion of the QBR—the Quality Business Review—we need to be sure to close the loop on how QBRs might look different by segment. Remember that we segmented our customers based on value and complexity? I have talked with many MSPs about assigning their segments as high-touch, mid-touch, or tech-touch. So the lowest tiered segment will get an automated version of a QBR.

Thinking back to the variables we considered in the first place, this makes a lot of sense. Imagine a small construction company and their technology needs. Investing time in quarterly reviews would be wasted on them and provide no additional value functionally or otherwise for your business. Instead automated, regular (maybe monthly) re-marketing emails can do three things:

1. Remind them that you have their best interests in mind and keep current with potential needs (highlighting new technologies)

2. Remind them that you are still supporting them if they have any new needs (ask discovery questions about their business needs as part of these communications)

3. Stay top of mind so competitors don't steal their attention because you are clearly taking care of them (and they can see the ROI)

This also means their renewal won't come as a surprise. Providing the same QBR information—even if only in an email or annually in a phone call—is then expected and appreciated.

QBRs truly are the hallmark of a Customer Success program. That said, other elements and processes like Recovery Plans and Referral Paths, and Products also play a part, which we discover in the next chapters.

Takeaways

> - Briefly cover what your customers already expect from their investment in working with you
>
> - QBRs are what sets you apart. Not just doing them, but the way in which you approach them. Focus on strategy.
>
> - You must reinforce the value of the investment that your customer has made with you
>
> - Resist the urge to be salesy

Chapter 9

Checklists and Processes Beyond the QBR

As you document the cadence of business reviews for each of your segments, it is important to also define other key components. Gainsight published a survey in 2019 benchmarking the most critical elements for a Customer Success program. The survey showed that the top three areas of focus for CSMs should be: increasing retention rates, driving revenue growth, and enhancing stack alignment/adoption. One interesting note is that Net Promoter Score (NPS) did not make the top five and Customer Satisfaction (CSAT) was actually at the bottom of the list.

A key for anyone who is handling Customer Success functions is that there can be no wasted communication. Always have a goal. You are there as a guide so you cannot go into any conversation just asking to "check in." That would not show that you know how to guide them to their next step. Instead, here are some conversation starters you can use to "check in" with a focus:

- "We have had some folks asking about..."

- "With _____ in the news, you might have concerns/questions about..."

- Make a specific statement around how you are helping companies with security, saving money, efficiency, impacting business goals.

Business owners are busy people. Check-ins without a purpose are not valued. Using this approach shows the owner that you value their time and understand their needs. This allows you to help set goals for their company. Owners invest in technology to grow their business. If you review their goals and have ideas, concerns, or questions related to them, you are on steady ground.

There are two other critical checklists or playbooks that CSMs need to have in their arsenal. These are recovery plans and referral paths.

Recovery plans

Imagine that Kerrie now regularly tracks and reports on customer health. This morning she notices that one of her high value/high complexity client's health has dropped from green to red. Kerrie can now pull out her recovery checklist and spring into action.

Recovery checklists/playbooks/processes vary by MSP. We have seen lots of iterations of this type of checklist. Some titles include: "Escalation process," "CPR process," and "Code Blue Checklist." Whatever you call them, ensure they get the job done.

Referral Path

Our MSP owner Paul has been able to delegate some work and now has time to focus on his Customer Success program. He has defined his high-touch, mid-touch, and tech-touch segments. He is less stressed and his clients are raving fans again.

Now that he has dedicated time to work on the business he is aiming to grow faster. His focus with CS to use the QBR process to drive upsells has worked well. He also well remembers the value of word-of-mouth advertising and referrals. In addition to using QBRs to make the referral "ask," he now targets his "green" customers (those with strong customer health scores) and develops goals to move them through the referral path checklist.

> "The most valuable advertising you can purchase can't be purchased directly. It comes from the care of your customers, creating super fans. From the moment they first hear of you, through the sales process, through every support interaction–you have the opportunity to develop these super fans of your company. When the opportunity arises to talk about an MSP, they will be able to go on for an hour about how great you treat them. They are, and always will be, your best salespeople. But your strategy to develop them has to be through building genuine empathy and caring into every phase of the customer journey."
>
> —Heather Johnson from Gozynta

MSPs who are uncomfortable asking for a referral typically feel that way because they feel like the favor is a big ask or inconvenience. Making the work on the end for your customer as easy as possible can help ease that feeling. Creating and outlining a process for asking for that referral makes it repeatable across your customer base and simplifies it for the customer.

Here's how one of my business partners would ask for referrals at a QBR:

> *"Mr/Mrs. Customer, I'm sure you know by now that I dislike pushy sales, but growing the business is part of my job... and you seemed like you got some real value from what we talked about today. Would you be willing to introduce me to someone else that you know who would see value in this sort of information about their business technology?"*

The rationale for this:

> "The hardest part is getting the words out—but you might just be surprised with the results If they say no, or that they aren't comfortable making an introduction, no worries—you win just by letting your customer know that if the opportunity arises that you'd appreciate a referral. But if you build a killer customer experience, deliver quality Business Reviews, and can bring yourself to ask all of your raving fans for a referral one to two times per year, you'll create a reliable drip of warm leads into your business."
>
> —Alex Farling, Former MSP
> Co-founder of Lifecycle Insights

There is no question that every MSP has its own unique flavor. Brainstorm or document other checklists/playbooks that non-Customer Success teams may run. Onboarding and offboarding are two examples that might be handled strictly by a technical team member.

Remember at the beginning when Paul kept everything in his head? It was very clear that it was not a process, let alone scalable. Imagine what he can delegate now that he has a documented process. Like many of our customers, Paul hired an intern to do some of the data, scheduling, and follow-up tasks, teeing up his time to tackle more strategic initiatives.

So here is a checklist on checklists:

- New client onboarding
- Customer recovery (CPR)
- Employee onboarding / offboarding
- New executive leadership CS Tasks
  & first impressions

- Prospect engagement process
- Sales process
- QBR process
- Client-facing fiscal EoY tasks

Now that we have wrestled the marshmallow that is *Process*, let's take a look at *Product*. Before you turn the page (Or did you cheat when you heard there was a product? I know how MSPs roll.) to find out what type of product should automate this work, know that the more the industry matures in terms of investing in Customer Success, the more products we will see. So let's define some criteria for what that product needs to do.

Takeaways

- Put a process/checklist in place for each repeatable task a CSM might run into

- Popular ones include:
  - New client onboarding
  - Customer recovery (CPR)
  - New employee onboarding / offboarding
  - New executive leadership CS Tasks & first impressions
  - Prospect engagement process
  - Sales process
  - QBR process
  - Client-facing fiscal EoY tasks

- Have a process in place to get referrals

CHAPTER 10

PRODUCT

I mentioned before and I'll say it again (and if you hear me on a webinar or podcast, I'll probably say it there too), Customer Success needs its own tool. It shouldn't use a sales tool and it shouldn't use a support tool.

This is bound to be controversial but why a sales tool designed to funnel prospects is called a CRM is beyond me. Let's dissect.

C for Customer
(nope, it's designed to be used with prospects)

R for Relationship
(we don't have one yet, that is why we need these notes)

M for Management
(OK, this one can stay)

I feel like you get what I am saying. We have a product for the sales team that is named suspiciously like it should be for the CSM team. And because of that, many, many... too many companies try to square peg/round hole it.

Due to this technological wolf in sheep's clothing, many CSMs are asked to track their work in CRMs. Not a fit.

CSMs need their own tool to track customer health in the same way sales can track progress toward hitting quota or support can track closing tickets. Customer Success is its own role, with its own people and process. They need their own product. Others agree:

> "Digital transformation of Customer Success is imminent. 83% of respondents think Customer Success should be the next function within their organization to undergo digital transformation."
>
> —*99Firms*

In the same way that you consult with your clients on their business needs before proposing technology, you should consider your priorities around Customer Success. Assess your company needs in the following areas:

1. Do you have actionable insights and visibility into your customer health?

2. Do you have a clear view of upsell opportunities?

3. Are you concerned that you don't track metrics around clients who have potential for churn?

4. Are easy-to-read reports available that show you how aligned clients are to your product stack?

5. Do you have a way to scale and automate your Customer Success program so that all clients get the service and partnership they want and deserve?

6. Are your QBRs as automated as possible?

Let's start with table-stakes—those features that are foundational to the work. A Customer Success platform for MSPs needs to:

1) Integrate with your PSA

This integration is key as it should pull contacts, companies, contracts, and assets. It should also push to/create tickets. These functions will ensure that the person in the Customer

Success role has all of the data that they need at their fingertips.

2) Allow the MSP to define and report on metrics around:

- Segmentation
- Health
- Opportunity

Flexibility in creation of these metrics allows the MSP to customize the platform to align with best practices for Customer Success *and* retain the best practices of the MSP that allows it to differentiate itself in the market.

3) Support the work of a CSM with an eye toward ease of use

A system designed for the Customer Success role should feel natural to the work it supports. Work-arounds and "hijacking" products not designed for this work will be costly in terms of effort. It should allow a user to create, document, and track progress toward goals and task completion.

4) Provide actionable insights and analytics

The platform needs to support both the day-to-day tactical work of the CSM and the strategic work. Dashboards should give insights to a Customer Success Manager's customer base and provide drill-through functions for easy reference and action.

5) Allow MSP-controlled user roles and permissions

It should allow the MSP to control role-based access. This will allow CSMs to have access to their client's data and for managers to have access across the company. These groups should be defined and controlled by the assigned MSP administrator(s) of the platform.

Takeaways

- CSMs need their own tool

- The tool needs to:

  - Integrate with the PSA
  - Report metrics on segmentation, health, and opportunity
  - Be easy to use
  - Provide fast insights with an eye toward actionable next steps
  - Allow MSPs to define user roles/permissions

PART 3
THE WHAT

Chapter 11

What Success Looks Like

So what does success look like in the day and the life of a CSM? It looks like data-driven, purpose-filled work. It starts weekly with a review. That review could be party of one or a team meeting, but it starts with the dashboard. There the Customer Success Manager identifies:

- Priority (High value) accounts who are at risk
- Upcoming QBRs
- Any carry-over tasks assigned to this week
- Prep work for scheduled QBRs
- Contract renewals

Any one of these bullets might mean one of 100 tactical to-do items, but having the data means you are focused on the right ones. That focus will help you address priorities that make an impact on business, both yours and theirs.

Done right, MSP owners or leaders of larger teams also have insights across their CSM's books of business. This is critical for forecasting within your own business.

This sounds perfect! But what do I do first?

1. Set goals for your business. Remember from the Datto study that MSPs grow twice as fast as their competitors by setting revenue targets around increasing MRR

2. Segment your client base

3. Set a cadence for QBRs and communications for each segment

4. Define and score the health of each of your clients

5. Track opportunities within each client

6. Use the data to define your path

Now that we have a focus, make way for Customer Success. CSMs run at their work like football blockers clearing paths for their clients. Starting with one new action will get the flywheel turning. The concept of the Flywheel Effect is that you stack effective actions to start the movement of the flywheel and it takes a life of its own. (For more details on the power of the Flywheel, check out *Good to Great* by Jim Collins.)

One of the best motivational talks I have ever heard was based on the philosophy of Sam Parker who wrote the book *212 The Extra Degree*. His core message was:

> "*At 211 degrees, water is hot. At 212 degrees, it boils. And with boiling water comes steam. And with steam you can power a locomotive. That extra degree makes all the difference.*"

So I encourage you to do one more thing. If you feel overwhelmed by "all the things," start with one. Prioritizing where you need to focus with relevant data is the place to start. Remember, going with your gut is not data.

CONCLUSION

Questions a CSM should be able to answer

If you think about the scenarios we have shared, the struggles and successes of Kerrie and Paul and our MSP partners, let's reflect on what questions CSMs need to answer to be most effective and proactive.

- How aligned are my accounts with our standards and practices?
- What opportunities are created by lack of alignment?
- What risks are created by lack of alignment?
- Which clients are at risk of churn?
- Which clients are at risk of churn due to a change in company leadership?
- Which clients represent an oversized share of our revenue, making their departure a more dire event?
- Where are my biggest opportunities?
- Which customers will I be meeting with in the near future?
- Which QBRs are scheduled and require prep?
- Who are my raving fans?

Getting buy-in

If you are saying, "This all sounds great but I am getting push-back internally," let's review. Way back in Chapter 1, we talked about the impact a strong Customer Success program can make. If you need to present your case on why Customer Success matters, here are the key takeaways:

- Customer Success programs make money (rather than cost money)
- CS drives customer loyalty and retention
- CS reduces churn (dramatically improving the financial impact in a valuation)
- CS increases customer referrals (thereby driving new business)
- CS gives your business better insights into your own business forecast and strategy
- CS differentiates your MSP by making strategic impact with your clients

So basically, a Customer Success program makes dollars and sense.

It is hard to make an argument against having a Customer Success program. (I mean we are talking about success here.) Yet some companies are still slow to implement. Here is a cautionary tale that I recently heard at a conference in case you are thinking of putting off refining your customer success program until later.

The MSP who was speaking had been jazzed to do a sales presentation for a prospect. In a discovery call, he learned what products and services they needed and the presentation went well. The CEO of the potential client said as much:

> "This is perfect. You offer all of the products and services we need—backups, anti-virus, dark web monitoring, etc. Send over your proposal and we will get back to you next week."

The next week the MSP received word that he lost the contract to the lowest bidder. Why? Because all the company evaluated was products and cost. On paper all of the MSPs looked the same. This MSP was so mad at himself because he had been so pleased to check all of the boxes that he forgot the human element and the strategic value he knew his company could bring to the table.

In hindsight, he believes that if he had talked about the business reviews and what a true strategic partnership looked like—including business continuity planning, budget forecasting, and proactive engagements—that he would have differentiated his company's value instead of losing based on cost.

If that resonates, then look back at your notes and decide where you need to start. If this sounds unlikely to you, I have a resource to help. There is an entire book on business consulting that can convince you otherwise. So before I go, I will add one more book to your reading list. *Getting Naked* by Peter Lencioni shows you how being a true strategic thought partner with both customers *and* prospects earn you raving fans and referrals even when you are the highest-priced option.

Now that we are ready to differentiate our business and act on Customer Success, let's consider a final thought on how to maximize our opportunities and profits with a platform solution that can deliver efficiency and value.

Products

Since the launch of Lifecycle Insights' QBR/vCIO platform in 2019, we have worked with hundreds of MSPs to define, refine, and scale their QBR process. As I have talked about here, that is foundational for MSPs regardless of their size.

Having run Customer Success for organizations of all sizes, I assumed that the world of Managed Services would have Customer Success platforms to support their work. We really scoured the internet to find such a tool. We ran into the usual suspects that were specifically built for the SaaS industry. If you are unfamiliar, here are some of the leaders in that space:

- Gainsight
- Kapta
- Totango

- PlanHat
- Churn Zero

We even found that some of our MSP partners were duct-taping these solutions to fit in with their process.

We really saw this need along with multiple requests from our partners to develop a solution for Customer Success unique to the MSP space (without the tremendous expense associated with the SaaS solutions). So that is exactly what we did.

This book comes to press as the Lifecycle Insights Customer Success platform is being released. We are betting that more companies will follow suit and start building this functionality. That is good for everyone. I have seen first hand how strong Customer Success programs can help grow and secure business. So as you further transform your CS program, be sure to use what you have learned here to define your needs and ensure you find a solution (be it Lifecycle Insights or another) to help you crush your goals.

I am insanely passionate about Customer Success. I have seen the impact across multiple industries and verticals. Managed Service Providers need to look forward, as pieces of the industry are further commoditized, to set themselves apart from their competition. This is done by truly partnering with customers to help them become overwhelmingly successful. Because success for them means success for you... Literally.

ACKNOWLEDGMENTS

If it takes a village to raise a child, it took all of that village plus my two children to deliver this book. I would like to thank many of them (and hope I didn't forget anyone).

Those two children, David and Josie, are fine young adults who are more than willing (and capable) to provide their mother with feedback. Josie also contributed with some graphics and marketing support. My husband, Frank, tolerated a summer of writing weekends in lieu of golf. I really have my parents to thank for somehow getting this math major to write.

I owe a great deal to Nick Coniglio for helping me wrestle the marshmallow of Customer Success to the ground from the very beginning. To him and our other co-founders, Alex Farling and Kurt Davis, thank you.

I was privileged to join a company as "the other Kellie 8o" and got rewarded with a friend and reviewer. To Woody Dillaha and Justin Serrano, who know Customer Success and how to build a program that makes an impact, I learned a great deal. To Beth Kawecki, Robin Fox, Justin Miller, Michele Robinson, Dan Calin, and Lori McAlister, for their support.

I am grateful that Nigel Moore of The Tech Tribe would take the time to provide feedback, resources, and a Foreword.

And now for a list of MSPs and MSP vendors who have partnered with us and provided great feedback for the book and Lifecycle Insights itself that has helped us grow and get better. (We do love our raving fans!)

Chris Wiser, Ray Orsini, Heather Johnson, Dave Sobel, Sean Lardo, Bob Coppedge, Matthew Fox, Jonathan Crowe, Elizabeth Copeland, Steve Kazan, Jennifer Bleam, Amy Morell, Lisa Shorr, Kevin Elsing, Raj Sidhu, and Ron Cotsoupolous

Props to Howard Globus for writing his own book and introducing me to his amazing editor, Demi Stevens. She can get a job done!

And lastly an apology to the folks on my street who thought "the new neighbor" walking with a clipboard was either neighborhood watch or an FBI agent (yep, they asked). And apologies for any errors, they are all mine.

Without further ado, I hope that you have found a nugget or two on ways to take actions toward scaling your Customer Success program. As we like to say: Happy Lifecycling!

ABOUT THE AUTHOR

Keep Calm
and let
Customer Success
handle it!

MARNIE STOCKMAN wanted to be a math teacher since 2nd grade. She loved the power of numbers and had a passion for helping others learn and grow. After graduating *summa cum laude* from Loyola University in Baltimore, MD, as a math major, she began teaching high school in Caroline County, MD.

After 7 years in the classroom, she became a stay-at-home mom for 7 years. Because 7 apparently is a magic number, she then became an administrator and then spent 7 years in Customer Success, becoming Sr. Director of Customer Success for a leading Ed Tech company (picking up her doctorate in Educational Leadership along the way).

Scaling Customer Success in those 7 years taught Marnie many things. One of which was that she cherished working with creative problem-solvers who enjoyed helping other businesses grow. She and a colleague set out to find a way to do that in a company of their own. This led them to another friend who owned an MSP and had a problem that the group could solve by building Lifecycle Insights.

The team at Lifecycle Insights unanimously made "grow raving fans" their number one core value. As their QBR/vCIO tool grew more and more raving fans, they saw a new need in the MSP space. There was a need for data, education (and humor never hurts) to help MSPs define, refine, and scale their Customer Success programs. The technical team began building an industry-disrupting Customer Success platform made for MSPs. And Marnie wrote the book on it, *Literally*.

When Marnie isn't Lifecycling, she can be found playing volleyball with her husband Frank and two twenty-somethings, David and Josie. (Or checking her email while repeatedly chasing a golf ball around).

Marnie believes you can attain success by working hard, using data, and killing 'em with kindness. She would love it if this book helped your MSP create a killer success program.

Made in the USA
Las Vegas, NV
20 April 2023

70850737R10075